SpringerBriefs in Business

SpringerBriefs present concise summaries of cutting-edge research and practical applications across a wide spectrum of fields. Featuring compact volumes of 50 to 125 pages, the series covers a range of content from professional to academic. Typical topics might include:

- A timely report of state-of-the art analytical techniques
- A bridge between new research results, as published in journal articles, and a contextual literature review
- A snapshot of a hot or emerging topic
- An in-depth case study or clinical example
- A presentation of core concepts that students must understand in order to make independent contributions

SpringerBriefs in Business showcase emerging theory, empirical research, and practical application in management, finance, entrepreneurship, marketing, operations research, and related fields, from a global author community.

Briefs are characterized by fast, global electronic dissemination, standard publishing contracts, standardized manuscript preparation and formatting guidelines, and expedited production schedules.

More information about this series at http://www.springer.com/series/8860

Bas Kodden

The Art of Sustainable Performance

A Model for Recruiting, Selection, and Professional Development

OPEN

 Springer

Bas Kodden
Nyenrode Business University
Breukelen, The Netherlands

ISSN 2191-5482   ISSN 2191-5490   (electronic)
SpringerBriefs in Business
ISBN 978-3-030-46462-2   ISBN 978-3-030-46463-9   (eBook)
https://doi.org/10.1007/978-3-030-46463-9

This Springer imprint is published by the registered company Springer Nature Switzerland AG
The registered company address is: Gewerbestrasse 11, 6330 Cham, Switzerland

Preface

"As a young man, it seemed that the American Billy Beane could beat anyone at any sport. As a natural, he was so much better than anyone he competed against, it almost seemed like he was playing a sport far easier than the one his opponents were playing. In his second year of high school, Billy Beane was both quarterback for the football team and point leader for the basketball team. It was as if he discovered talents in himself before his body was ready to do anything with them. For example, he was able to dunk a ball before his hands were even big enough to lift the ball with one hand. Billy was a typical example of an American teenager with many talents, including a major one: playing baseball" (Lewis 2003).

Swarms of Scouts

With the exception of football, baseball is the most popular sport in the United States, America's favorite pastime. It is more popular than basketball, hockey, tennis, and many times bigger than soccer.

It should come as no surprise then that Billy Beane was blessed with wonderful expectations for his future. His talents, particularly in this very popular sport, seemed a guarantee for success.

Not only did Billy have many talents, but he also had the right body physique. At just fourteen years of age, he already towered over his own father by 7 inches. This allowed Billy to stand his ground against much older players. In his first year in high school, his coach even let him pitch in the last game of the season, despite protests by older teammates. Billy got no points against, struck out 10 batters, and even managed to score two hits in four innings. In his second year, he achieved an unbelievably high batting average in one of the toughest high school divisions in the country. Starting his third year, Billy's height measured 6'5" and he weighed an impressive 180 pounds. By then, major league scouts were turning up to each of his games. In his first official game as a pro, he only allowed two hits as a pitcher, stole four bases as a batter, and scored three hits. These statistics remained a Californian record for his age group even decades later.

Kiss of Death

It was not difficult for Billy to stand out. In the eyes of all scouts, he was a true winner. A major talent, with the right physique and looks. They all saw what they so desperately wanted to see: a child prodigy, a *Wunderkind*. The greatest talents in history are often described as child prodigies. Kids with an almost supernatural ability to excel at what they do.

Some examples are Wolfgang Mozart, Tiger Woods, or more recently, young Dutch Formula 1 driver, Max Verstappen. All of them appeared to have enormous talents from a very young age. But something else was going on in the case of Billy Beane. Despite being a natural at baseball, it did not seem to offer him much joy. Billy skipped practice, arrived late, or was sloppy with his exercises. More and more, Billy started slacking.

Still, the professional baseball scouts continued to see what they wanted to see: a young prodigy who was destined to become the greatest in a sport that by then had practically no more financial limits in the United States. Teams paid astronomical sums for players that would draw people to their stadiums. Billy was destined for fame and glory and everyone wanted to be part of it. Blinded by bias and the chance of financial gain, the scouts missed crucial indications that Billy might not become the baseball great they expected him to be. Billy Beane had received his *kiss of death* long before. He was fine with it. "I never looked at Billy's stats", a scout admitted years later. "I simply did not have to. He had everything."

"Billy was a talent wearing a mask", according to Roger Jongewaard, head scout for the Mets. "There are great guys and there are top guys. Billy was the absolute top. He had the physique, the speed, the arm; he had it all. He was a true athlete. Not to mention the fact that he got good grades and dated the prettiest girls. He was charming; he could be whatever he wanted."

And that is where Jongewaard and his colleagues went wrong. Billy did not really want to play baseball all that badly, he wanted to go to college. Billy wanted to go to Stanford. Receiving a college education was his main goal.

Logic, Science, and Baseball

Ten years after his—to many completely unexpected—decision to quit professional baseball (1989), Billy returned to the sport. First as a scout and later as general manager for his former team, the Oakland A's. Although Billy had vowed never again to make a decision based on money, he once again ended up in a world where everything was centered on money. Where to find it, where to spend it, and above all, on who to spend it! The major league was all about attracting and selecting the right talent. It still is.

The talent scouts for the Oakland A's, with whom Billy had to work together, turned out to be no different to their predecessors who had deemed Billy Beane a future star baseball player. Just like before, they were the ones who decided who would be recruited and be allowed to play ball. As general manager, Billy decided to do without their "professional insights". At that time, scouts were still focused on high school players, particularly high school pitchers. After all, their young arms were fresh and they were able to deliver the only performance the scouts could measure and quantify how fast their pitch was. But Billy knew that the most important trait for a pitcher was not his physical strength, but his ability to strike out his opponents. This can be achieved in a number of ways.

Billy Beane knew that you only had to look at statistics to recognize that high school pitchers had half the chance of making it to the big leagues compared to college pitchers. A quarter in the case of position players. But what happened when you would simply let the scouts have their way? They would only select high school pitchers in the first round and you ended up having to pay millions to sign them! It mocked the laws of probability and it mocked the laws of logic. Logic—perhaps even science—was the aspect that Billy Beane really wanted to introduce to baseball. Scouts, who were often former players, had the tendency to be overly influenced by a player's recent performance and only saw what they wanted to see. However, past performance is no guarantee for future results and nothing is what it seems. Billy Beane knew that from his own experience. After all, he had been at the top of all those little lists.

Billy had started to realize that the scouting and selecting of baseball players were in the same stage of development as medical science was in the eighteenth century. Billy and his future right-hand man, Harvard statistician Paul DePodesta, became fascinated by that irrationality, because as they saw it, whoever managed to put an end to that irrationality, would create great opportunities for themselves.

A True Winner

Billy Beane was different and thought differently. Winning was all that mattered. Billy's first pick was the unknown David Beck, who he offered a contract based solely on data provided by his own statistician, Paul Podesta. When he did his warm-up, it was the most bizarre thing anyone had ever seen. When David Beck drew back his left arm, his left hand would flop around like he had no wrist. It was almost like his hand was about to come loose and fly away. David Beck suffered from hyper-mobility and might even have been considered handicapped.

From that moment on, Beck was no longer known as David Beck to the scouts. They started calling him "The Creature". The Creature subsequently dominated the rookie league. With his "Halloween Hand" and his 84-miles-an-hour fastball, he was so much better than his opponents that they had no idea what was happening to them.

Paul's computer would spit out many more unknown players who were offered contracts. Billy took away the recruiting tasks from the scouts and gave them to people who had what he valued most: an academic background in something other than baseball. They could look at baseball from a different perspective. A perspective that was not just based on a gut-feeling or expectation, but on actively looking for indicators that could predict sustainable performance.

The story about Billy Beane and the movie *Moneyball*, starring Brad Pitt as the general director of the poor but successful baseball team the Oakland A's, was a major inspiration for writing this book and researching performance indicators and personality traits for sustainable performance. A quest for specific characteristics to explain our own sustainable performance.

Billy Beane wanted to win the major league with his baseball team. While others were competing for players with high batting averages or hit numbers, he dove into the statistics and combined unique players into a winning team.

Utrecht, The Netherlands   Bas Kodden

Reference

Lewis M (2003) Moneyball. The art of winning an unfair game. Writers House, New York, NY, www.verenigdestaten.info

Acknowledgements

"The greatest part of a writer's time is spent in reading. In order to write; a man will turn over half a library to make one book," Samuel Johnson once said. I want to give special thanks to all authors and colleagues who inspired me to write this book.

Christel, Sep, and Tom. I could barely stop writing. I simply couldn't let the book go, it had to be finished. Since 2014, not a day went by that I did not think of the book. Thank you for your patience. I love you!!

Thank you to all participants in this research. You made it possible for me to complete this study. Thank you to my publisher Vakmedianet for your guidance and your faith. Special thanks to Gerri Reimert, without who this book would never have existed. Writing isn't something you do on your own, people often say. That was certainly true in this case.

And thanks to everyone who played a part in finishing the book—my own Zeigarnik effect. I can finally let it go.

Introduction

Abstract How are individuals and organizations able to continue winning? How does one team go from victory to victory? What is the secret to their success? Many companies struggle to achieve high levels of performance. Many more struggle to sustain them. While managers set organizational targets or attempt to implement new strategies or actions that improve their performance, the common result is a slew of unfinished projects, disengaged employees, and disappointing results. Which organizational concepts and individual elements can be linked to the ability of professionals to deliver sustainable performance, both in a team and on an individual level? In this study, a total of over 1100 professionals were assessed on their level of talent for their jobs, the level to which they matched twelve personality traits, three elements of work engagement, three aspects of organizational fit, the level to which they met the physical and mental requirements of their job, and the level to which they had demonstrated sustainable performance—both as individuals and in teams—in recent years.

Keywords Personality traits · Key performance indicators ·
Work engagement · Sustainable performance

Introduction

Past performance is no guarantee for future results. The book and movie *Moneyball* drew a lot of attention in the United States. The idea of alternative hiring procedures and statistics-based recruiting and selection procedures had a huge impact. What is needed to continue performing at a high level? How can you reinvent yourself as an individual, as a team, and as an organization in order to stay successful?

Fifteen years of being an entrepreneur, for me, it ended in 2013. Over thirty thousand hours of hard work, of falling and getting back up again. They were also 15 years of study and research, finally resulting in a Ph.D. (Kodden 2011). What had started with the goal to improve my own business—after all, nothing is as practical as a good theory (Lewin 1951)—ended years later working for Nyenrode Business University, where I teach ambitious professionals in the fields of leadership, entrepreneurship, and personal development.

Time to Take Stock

What had I truly learned after all those years of practice and study, and which theories had I found to be genuinely important? This question, which I asked myself during a break between teaching MBA students in 2013, hit me like a ton of bricks. What was really the essence of it all? During my time as an entrepreneur, why did some things go right while other things failed? What had brought me joy? And did all that theoretical knowledge I had come across over the years have anything to do with reality?

I had just finished explaining the ten thousand hours theory to my students. In his book, *Outliers* (2009), American best-selling author, Malcolm Gladwell, supports the statement by Swedish psychologist Ericsson (2014, 2016) that you can only gain insights into personal success after you have spent at least ten thousand hours practicing something. By 2013, I had three times that, both in acquired knowledge as well as in terms of practical experience. It was time for me to take stock.

Gladwell's book and Ericsson's ten thousand hours theory became the reason for me to write the book *Become a HERO* (2014). Something I really enjoyed. In it, I tried to find my own answers to questions such as What management theories are truly valuable in the real world? Which organization and management aspects increase job satisfaction? *Become a HERO* turned out to be a hit, particularly, because it seemed that many professionals in the Netherlands were not satisfied with their job. Many lacked (and still lack) work engagement and life engagement and, like me, were looking for tools to achieve those.

What is Needed to Continue Performing?

As a researcher, an entrepreneur, but especially as a father to two young children, there was one question that kept me awake at night: What is needed to continue performing? After all, winning once is not good enough. As an entrepreneur, I had employed hundreds of people, conducted or had others conduct over a thousand interviews, and tested hundreds of talented people. Nevertheless, I still often felt that maybe I had hired the wrong person. Even worse, how many talented individuals had I let slip through my fingers who had the abilities and personality traits to become top performers that would have significantly contributed to my teams and organization? Had I been blinded, focused too much on myself, or had I put too much stock in appearances? Why was it that I—as an entrepreneur or person—lacked the skills to truly recognize who was talented and who was not?

What is needed to continue performing? Unanswered questions like that continued to make me restless. How you could become attached to and remain engaged in your work, sure, that was something that I had figured out. By making available the right energy sources, an energetic attitude, taking charge of your own life, and above all *taking action*, that is what brings results. But how do you make sure that you can win *again*? And again after that? What is needed for that? And how do you recognize candidates that have the right knowledge and ability?

The question I asked myself in late 2013, after reading *Moneyball* (2003), and watching the movie, was this: Which personality traits and performance criteria are crucial for our sustained performance? And what was the fatherly advice that I could give my two young children? With the results, I could also answer what is the most crucial question for many businesses: How and based on what criteria can you select the best people for your team and organization? All in order to keep on winning.

The Journey, Not the Destination

I went looking for answers, devoured dozens of management books and scientific articles, spoke to experts from academic, professional sports and business circles and created a model that I thought could explain the importance of personality traits; a model that could also explain why I myself had not always performed optimally in my own life.

You've probably been there yourself. After years of learning, studying, and preparing, you started your first job. Ignorant, unaware, and perhaps not quite competent yet, but with boundless energy that you were finally going to put to use. You received your first compliments, got your first promotion, and started off on a high. Fantastic, I had it in me all the time, you said to yourself. Nobody saw it, but now they do, my talent is finally getting noticed. I have arrived. I just had to discover it. Right?

However, things often get difficult after graduating or winning an award. Because you wonder what's next. I realized later that it is not about the award or diploma. What I really enjoyed was getting there. The flow, the enthusiasm that comes with a new challenge and pursuing a new goal. Life engagement is not about the destination, about the goal; it is about the journey. Which personality traits will be the most helpful to you during that journey? Exactly, that is what this book is about!

Past Performance

Just like Billy Beane, we all receive our own *kiss of death* at one time or another (Friedman 2011). We've all had our first successes and celebrated them, but then the first cracks start to appear and you notice that there are many other individuals who are just as good—if not better. That first win in no way guarantees another win tomorrow. Many department heads, managers, board members, CEOs, and entrepreneurs have also experienced this phenomenon from the perspective of leaders. One team was successful, while another did not do so well. And the team and organization that were once so successful suddenly started to show disappointing performances years later. Poor performances that could not be explained by the economy, competition, or anything else. Things simply didn't work anymore.

"Talent is time-sensitive," according to fellow professor van der Sluis (2008, 2009). "It is transient. You can be considered very talented one day, people love you and want to network with you, but all of that can change in an instant. You can fall off your pedestal. Take professional athletes, for instance. The more games and trophies they win, the more people love them. However, expectations also increase. It is easier to learn how to win than to keep on winning. Success never simply occurs out of nowhere and quality is never a coincidence."

"Past performance is no guarantee for future results," as many of today's financial radio and TV ads say. Unfortunately, that statement is also true for our own lives and careers. But which personality traits and which employees do you then need in order to remain successful? Whenever I spoke about this topic with experts from academia or professional sports, I often heard a thing like, "It's a matter of perseverance," or "Enthusiasm determines everything."

That seemed obvious, hard to argue, but I thought there had to be more. And, as Billy Beane, the legendary baseball coach from Oakland found out, there is indeed more. Much more. The movie *Moneyball,* about his personality and drive to discover the most important performance indicators in baseball, inspired me to start a similar study. Instead, mine would be aimed at the current personality traits and performance indicators of Dutch professionals.

Culture of Mediocrity

Whether we like it or not, the Dutch culture of only doing the bare minimum no longer suffices. A Harvard diploma is within the reach of many these days. In 2008, there were 179,800 Chinese students who received education abroad. By 2015, that number had already grown to 523,700, an impressive increase of 13.9% compared to the year before (Rammeloo 2016).

According to the Institute for International Education, 27% of them went to school in the USA and 20% in the UK. Especially prestigious universities such as Harvard, Columbia, and New York University are popular. Of the 9396 international students that were enrolled at Harvard in 2016, 938 were from China. A year's tuition for one of those schools costs upward of 50,000 dollars, but many upper-middle-class Chinese people are more than willing to pay it. The American universities welcome them with open arms. In 2014, Chinese students added 10 billion dollars to their income. Tuition is not even the biggest expense for many Chinese students. They also spend tens of thousands of dollars on coaching and training to prepare them for their future careers.

The job market has changed completely because of a new generation full of young, ambitious, and very well-educated professionals from all over the globe who want their piece of the pie. And they often get it, at the expense of our own young professionals, who often think the bare minimum is good enough.

Therefore, I believe that modern parents should not just raise their kids with love and attention in a safe and nurturing environment, but also make them more resilient. To prepare them for a job market where they will be confronted with high demands on performance. Of course, giving them love and attention comes first, but preparing them for what the future will demand from them, should definitely be next on the list. But how do we do that? And more importantly, what are the requirements?

Moneyball

The story of Billy Beane, reinventing yourself, the movie adaptation of *Moneyball* starring Brad Pitt and a chance to meet one of Billy Beane's best friends, were the reasons for my own research. My own *Moneyball*: Why and based on what criteria are certain talented people in the Netherlands hired while others are rejected? What personality traits do continually successful Dutch professionals have? Do we perhaps all have the same blind spot when it comes to finding the right candidate? (Kodden 2014).

The result of three years of research now lies before you. Eighteen months of preparation and two years of actual research among supervisors and senior colleagues of over 1100 professionals and many dozens of interviews with experts from science, business, and sports sectors provided new insights that can help you reinvent yourself as a professional and help build sustainably performing organizations.

I hope you will enjoy the book!

Bas Kodden

References

Ericsson KA (ed) (2014) The road to excellence: the acquisition of expert performance in the arts and sciences, sports, and games. Psychology Press, New York, NY

Ericsson KA (2016) Peak: secrets from the new science of expertise. Houghton Mifflin Harcourt, Boston, MA

Friedman WJ (2011) The Zeigarnik effect and completing everything

Gladwell M (2009) Outliers: the story of success. Little, Brown and Company, New York, NY

Kodden SFGP (2011) Dedication. A study to analyse the effects of organizational design on employee engagement and knowledge productivity within Dutch legal service firms. Nyenrode Business Universiteit, Breukelen

Kodden S (2014) Be a HERO. How to bring out leadership in everyone. Bernard Daniel Press

Kodden SFGP and Van Ingen R (2019) Time for a new E/RA. J Appl Bus Econ 21(4):71–84

Lewin K (1951) Field theory in social science; selected theoretical papers (ed D. Cartwright). Harper & Row, New York, NY

Lewis M (2003) Moneyball. The art of winning an unfair game. Writers House, New York, NY

Rammeloo E (2016) Chinezen azen op plekje aan Amerikaanse universiteit

van der Sluis LEC (2008) Talent Management in strategisch perspectief. Nyenrode Business University, Breukelen

van der Sluis LEC and Berkhout B (2009) Nederland Talentenland. Themanummer Develop 1:4–7

Contents

About the Author

Bas Kodden is a writer, speaker, and researcher in the field of leadership, entrepreneurship, and personal development. Work engagement is one of his most important focus areas.

- www.sebastiaankodden.com
- @BasKodden
- @SebastiaanKodden
- @SebastiaanKodden
- bas@kodden.net
- +31 30 2611061

Chapter 1
The Importance of Sustainable Development

Abstract The success of organizations with many knowledge workers, such as law firms, insurance companies, and accounting firms, is assumed to be depending on the quality, performance, and engagement of the knowledge workers themselves. To quote Davenport (2002): "In the current economy, they are the horses that pull the plow of economic progress. If our companies are going to be more profitable, if our strategies are going to be successful, it will be because our knowledge workers did their work in a more productive and efficient manner." But how can organizations be successful in engaging and retaining their knowledge workers and avoid the risk of attrition of their best employees?

Keywords Performance indicators · Recruiting · Selection · Work engagement · Sustainable performance

1.1 Introduction

The same thing that happened with Billy Beane's scouts (Lewis 2003), seems to be happening in our world. Research shows that candidates are selected mostly based on the estimated talent, past achievements, and characteristics that their (new) employers—often subconsciously—see in themselves (UvA 2008). The results are alarming. Even today, it turns out that 88% of Dutch professionals are not fully engaged when it comes to their jobs (Kodden 2014). What makes it even worse is that levels of engagement appear to be declining. Less than 77% of all Dutch employees indicate that they are happy in their job, 5% of the Dutch workforce is currently suffering a burnout and another 13% is close to it. Today, more people are not working because of mental health issues than physical illnesses (Kodden 2011; Kodden and Van Ingen 2019).

A hundred years after Frederick Taylor, we are still dulling each other's intrinsic motivation. A few years ago, a large poll carried out by Gallup among 230,000 employees from 142 countries showed that only 13% felt engaged at work. The Netherlands scored even worse than average: only 9% were genuinely enthusiastic about their job (Gallup 2013). According to psychologist Barry Schwartz, 90% of adults spend half their waking lives on things they would rather not be doing and in places where they would rather not be (Schwarz 2016).

According to the Chartered Institute of Personnel and Development (CIPO), the costs of a mismatch between vacancy and candidate are equal to two-and-a-half annual salaries of that person. In one of its studies, Harvard Business School even calculated an amount three to five times the annual salary. Even ten times in the case of highly specialized positions or generalist top-level positions in an organization.

This shows that just as a cost consideration, it is important to overlook as little as possible when it comes to recruitment and selection of new talent. And that does not even include all the potential social and personal consequences. Another issue is the number of candidates that miss out on suitable jobs and great opportunities, simply because the wrong candidate was hired.

1.2 Intrinsic Motivation

"When you let those numbers sink in, you realize how much ambition and energy we are currently leaving on the shelf," writes Bregman (2016). Imagine if we all committed to each other's intrinsic motivation. That would mean a major revolution. CEOs would do their jobs because they believed in their companies, scientists would put in long hours simply out of curiosity, and teachers would teach because they'd feel a responsibility towards their students. Psychologists would keep treating their patients as long as it takes and bankers would get their satisfaction from their role as a service provider. Professionalism and competence would be paramount, not efficiency, and productivity. However, this requires a completely different approach to talent and performance management (Knegtmans 2016). One that supposes: "Talent is good, but character is better."

As was previously concluded by researchers from the University of Amsterdam in a large-scale study together with Randstad, Dutch CEOs and recruiters mainly look for talent, experience, and specific knowledge and skills (UvA 2008). Although this approach seems useful for clearly defined jobs, we should be aware that jobs and job requirements change over time.

Knowledge expires quickly—and is expiring more quickly all the time—yet new knowledge and skills seem crucial in today's rapidly changing market. Supervisors and HR specialists should, therefore, pay more attention to their candidates' personalities, i.e. their mental capabilities, specific personality traits, and sustainable employability (UvA 2008).

1.3 Successful Selection

On the basis of extensive research carried out by Schmidt and Hunter (1998) and others, we can conclude that certain selection methods will yield more information about candidates than others. Because the results of Schmidt and Hunter are based on large, international, and random testing, their article is still the basis for many studies on recruitment and selection methods today. Researchers from the University of Amsterdam reached similar conclusions in 2008. The methods that provide the best insight into an applicant's capabilities are the verifiable task achievements of the candidate (which requires the employee to have been working and performing within the organization for some time), an aptitude test that tests mental abilities and a structured selection interview. An individual's references are poor indicators of their future performance (UvA 2008).

"Get the right people on the bus," was the most important advice of management expert Jim Collins in his book *Good to Great* (2001). One of the participants in the Sports Leadership Program where I teach, Max Caldas, coach of the Dutch men's field hockey team, expressed it as follows: "You are the average of the people around you." But then what traits are the decisive factors for professionals who manage to keep performing, and how do you select them?

1.4 Performance Indicators and Selection Criteria

My very own *Moneyball* (2003) was born. I began a study on performance indicators and personality traits among over 1100 professionals, three times the required sample size. I included over twenty performance indicators in a research model based on five general concepts that I had mapped out after consulting with scientific and professional sports experts, studying scientific articles, and reading many different management books.

These five general concepts related to the importance of the following:

1. the degree of talent present;
2. the degree of presence of certain personality traits;
3. the degree of fit with the organization;
4. the degree of work engagement;
5. the degree of fit with the (physical and mental) requirements.

These concepts and their individual elements were linked to the ability of professionals to deliver sustainable performance, both in a team and on an individual level. Delivering sustainable performance is defined in this study as *being able to repeatedly achieve personal and team goals*.

The aforementioned concepts are visualized in the research model shown in Fig. 1.1.

I decided to use this research model to ask supervisors and senior employees how they would rate random employees or coworkers (with answers such as: totally agree, agree, neither agree nor disagree, disagree and totally disagree) using questions such as:

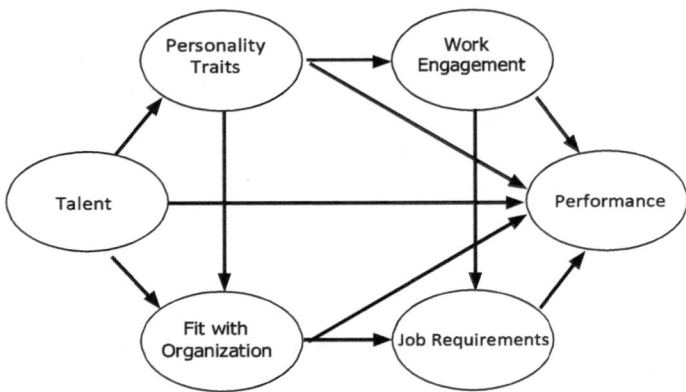

Fig. 1.1 The research model

- Compared to his or her co-workers, this employee has on average much less/less/neither less nor more/more/much more natural talent and innate predisposition to excel at his or her job.
- Compared to his or her co-workers this employee has on average much less/less/neither less nor more/more/much more willpower to excel.
- This employee has above-average intrinsic motivation to excel.
- This employee has above-average confidence in difficult situations.

1.5   Research Model and Questions

The model resulted in the following six research questions:

1. To what degree is talent important for sustainable performance by professionals?
2. To what degree are certain personality traits important for sustainable performance by professionals?
3. To what degree is work engagement important for sustainable performance by professionals?
4. To what degree do physical and mental job requirements influence sustainable performance by professionals?
5. To what degree is a good fit with the organization important for sustainable performance by professionals? And finally,
6. To what degree does the applied research model have a good statistical fit, and can it be used as a framework for talent development, and recruitment and selection services?

Following this methodology, a total of over 1100 professionals were assessed on their level of talent for their jobs, the level to which they matched twelve personality traits, three elements of work engagement, three aspects of organizational fit, the level to which they met the physical and mental requirements of their job, and the level to which they had demonstrated sustainable performance—both as individuals and in teams—in recent years.

The performance indicators selected related to the level of:

1.   talent;
2.   willpower (personality traits);
3.   self-control(personality traits);
4.   intrinsic motivation(personality traits);
5.   extrinsic motivation(personality traits);
6.   optimism (personality traits);
7.   self-esteem (personality traits);
8.   ability to cope with stress (personality traits);
9.   self-efficacy (personality traits);
10. adaptability (personality traits);
11. self-confidence (personality traits);
12. intelligence (personality traits);
13. ambition (personality traits);
14. vitality (work engagement);
15. absorptive capacity (work engagement);
16. dedication (work engagement);
17. fit with the job (fit with the organization);
18. fit with the corporate culture (fit with the organization);
19. fit with the management style(fit with the organization);
20. fit with the physical job requirements (job requirements);
21. fit with the mental job requirements (job requirements).

I always ask people attending my classes and lectures the following question: Which personality traits do you think are the most important for sustainable performance? I asked over fifty Dutch CEOs a similar question: "Which of these personality traits would you use to select new employees?" Could it be the case that our leaders consciously or perhaps unconsciously use the same hiring criteria as the personality traits that this study has shown to be so important? If so, this would mean there was a perfect match and it would provide the right candidates with the right opportunities.

This Book Provides:

• An explanation of the most relevant scientific insights regarding talent and other personality traits for recruitment and selection and sustainable performance.
• The results of a large-scale study among supervisors and senior employees on the talent and other personality traits of over 1100 professionals.
• The results of practical research into the chosen selection criteria among over 50 CEOs and managing directors. Do their visions match with the results of previous scientific research?
• New insights, frameworks, models, and tools to reinvent yourself and select the best candidates for your organization.

1.6   Structure of the Book

In the following chapters, I will discuss several of the performance indicators and personality traits that have been introduced. I will deal with the most important performance indicators and personality traits but will also include several performance indicators and personality traits that have turned out to be less important for sustainable performance than previously assumed. I furthermore discuss the performance indicators and personality traits that Dutch CEOs think are crucial in the hiring of new employees, but which have proven to be of lesser importance. In addition to the results of this study, I will also include the findings of other scientists and management authors regarding these aspects.

After I have described the results of my study, I will discuss what these performance indicators essentially have in common: the positive consequences of the Zeignarnik effect. I will explain what this is, where it comes from, and how you can use it to your advantage. Finally, I will provide you with several tools that can be used to improve yourself and more efficiently find the best candidate for a position in your organization. Detailed results and the justification of my research methodology can be found in the appendices.

1.7   On a Final Note

Please keep one thing in mind before you get started. This book and the research behind it are not the result of a quest for the holy grail of sustainable performance. Every study, including mine, has its limitations, requiring a certain level of caution and restraint in its conclusions. The study was conducted with the utmost care, but it should be acknowledged this study may have been influenced by the respondents' bias and their socially acceptable answers. Although this study has provided important insights, many studies have methodological issues that call into question the reliability and validity of their conclusions. For instance, it is not possible to make any statements about causality based on cross-sectional research. Experimental research is sometimes defined by limited generalizability in terms of actual work environments. The results of this study should, therefore, be taken merely as a guide and can only be considered an inspiration to act.

References

Bregman R (2016) Weg met control. Leve de intrinsiek gemotiveerde mens. De Correspondent, 18 Oct 2016. Consulted at www.decorrespondent.nl

Collins J (2001) Good to great. Why some companies make the leap … and other's don't. William Collins

Davenport T (2002) Can you boost knowledge work's impact on the bottom line? Manage Update 7(11):3–5

Gallup (2013) Worldwide, 13% of employees are engaged at work. http://www.gallup.com/poll/165269/worldwide-employees-engaged-work.aspx

Knegtmans R (2016) Agile Talent. Negen cruciale stappen bij de selectie van het toptalent van morgen. Business Contact, Amsterdam

Kodden SFGP (2011) Dedication. A study to analyse the effects of organizational design on employee engagement and knowledge productivity within Dutch legal service firms. Nyenrode Business Universiteit, Breukelen

Kodden S (2014) Be a HERO. How to bring out leadership in everyone. Bernard Daniel Press

Kodden SFGP, Van Ingen R (2019) Time for a new E/RA. J Appl Bus Econ

Lewis M (2003) Moneyball. The art of winning an unfair game. Writers House, New York, NY

Schmidt F, Hunter J (1998) The validity and utility of selection methods in personnel psychology: practical and theoretical Implications of 85 years of research findings. Psychol Bull 124(2):262–274

Schwarz B (2016) Waarom we werken. Amsterdam University Press, Amsterdam

UvA (2008) Personeelsselectie in tijden van krapte. Diemen, Onderzoek door UvA en Randstad)

Chapter 2
Talent as Precursor for Performance

Abstract Giving direction to your life is only possible when you work towards high, authentic objectives with complete dedication. By doing those things where your unique talents and interests intersect. Live an engaged life and you will live a happy life, according to the Work Engagement Theory which I had studied all those years. I realized that after fifteen years of practical experience this is easier said than done.

Keywords Talent · Work engagement theory · Sustainable performance

2.1 Introduction

You cannot expect performance without talent. That seems obvious. The main question that had kept nagging at me all those years became the first research question for a three-year study: "To what extent is talent important and responsible for actual performance?" This was my first hypothesis:

Hypothesis 1
Having talent leads to (better) performance (Fig. 2.1).

2.2 The Concept of "Talent"

But what exactly is talent? No matter how many books on the talent you read, none provide a clear scientific definition of this ubiquitous concept. According to some, it is about the smartest people, or the ones with the best educations, or people with the

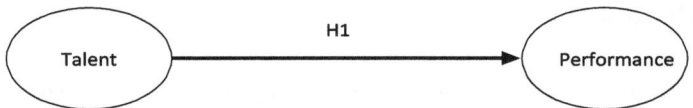

Fig. 2.1 Hypothesis

most relevant experience. Some organizations even apply the word "talent" to their entire workforce, making the term essentially meaningless.

"Talent" is also used to describe certain phenomena, like: "The War on Talent has begun." According to the Dutch dictionary, the *Dikkevan Dale* talent is "The natural giftedness to excel at something." This definition has also been used in this study, the natural giftedness and innate aptitude that allow a professional to excel in his or her job.

2.3 Talent Is Overrated

Talent Is Overrated is the title of Geoff Colvin's best seller (2010), in which he demonstrates how we have been looking at the concept of talent in the wrong way for years. In recent decades, more and more research has become available that unequivocally proves that talent is seriously 'overrated'. In fact, some even claim that it does not matter at all. The concept of talent remains important, however. After all, how we view talent determines our actions, how we stimulate our children, and it is the basis for how we apply ourselves or our employees. Therefore, a clear understanding of and research into the importance of talent remains extremely valuable.

An example is the psychologist Ericsson (2014, 2016). He has been studying the exceptional performance by chess champions, athletes, child prodigies, and musical geniuses. Together with a science journalist, he wrote an overview of his findings. The book, titled *Peak: Secrets form the New Science of Expertise* (2016), shows that if you want to excel at something, you need the dedication to keep trying and practicing. What is most surprising about Ericsson's study is that, according to him, talent does not actually exist. He says that what we generally refer to as talent, is nothing more than everything we have learned. According to the professor of psychology at Florida State University, the only true talent is something that we all have, the ability to learn.

But does that mean that there is no such thing as aptitude or innate talent? Ericsson is clear: "As a scientist, you cannot just say that something does not exist. But I have yet to meet someone who could do something special right away without any practice. In all those years, I never came across a single case of exceptional talent that could not be plausibly explained by practice (Meijers 2016)." My first hypothesis is, "having talent leads to (better) performance." But to what extent does that apply? And what do Dutch CEOs and supervisors think about the issue? The conclusion of this chapter will provide the most important results of my research.

2.4 Individuals Who Excel

Thousands of studies on talent, including the one by Galton (2018)—a distant cousin to the thirteen years older Charles Darwin—show that performance by excelling individuals, who at first glance appeared very talented, was not so much the result of talent, but rather of other factors. Factors such as personal focus and training. Children who were able to read at a very young age had not inherited that talent from their parents, but rather from their personal dedication to wanting to read at a young age. Studies showed that the same was true for "gifted" musicians, tennis players, swimmers, and mathematicians. Time after time, environmental influences turned out to determine success, not some impressive talent (Colvin 2010)!

But what about Mozart? How could his achievements not be viewed as the result of a major talent? After all, he wrote his first compositions when he was five and his first symphony when he was just eighteen! A child prodigy, people said. But as research has shown, even in the case of Mozart, his talent—if that even exists—only became valuable when he was given a lot of time to receive instruction and practice for developing his skills. Children of parents who do not play any instruments can still develop their musical skills, but few reach the top, other studies show (Colvin 2010; Syed 2011). Many musicians, who did reach the top, did so by studying and practicing music from an early age.

The same was true for Mozart. His father, Leopold Mozart, was already an accomplished composer in his own day. In addition, he turned out to be a very domineering parent, who started his son on an intensive program of composing and playing at just three years old. Leopold was a renowned pedagogue and published his handbook for violin teaching in the same year that Mozart was born. His most important student had arrived. From a very young age, Wolfgang Mozart received intensive guidance from an expert, who even lived in the same house. Even so, his performances were out of this world, right? Isn't he is known as a child prodigy for a reason? Still, the old adage is true here as well; nothing is what it seems!

Many of young Wolfgang's manuscripts eventually turned out not to actually be his own. His father had corrected them over and over again and added to them long before anyone else got to see them, later studies showed. Father Leopold even stopped composing his own works from the time he started guiding young Mozart.

Many of young Mozart works turned out not to be his own. At best, they can be considered the result of a team effort. His first masterpiece that has been recognized as truly his, is his piano concertono.9 (KV271). But by then "little Mozart" was already 21 years of age and could hardly be considered a child (prodigy). A genius, however, yes, that he was (Colvin 2010).

And what about Tiger Woods? Some people who have studied performance excellence have called him "the Mozart of golf." The backgrounds of both these "child prodigies" show surprising parallels. Tiger Woods' father, Earl, was an educator who taught young children and had a passion for sports. Earl Woods wrote a generally unknown book titled, *Training a Tiger* (1997).

During his own childhood, Earl had been a pretty good baseball player. In the years before Tiger was born, however, he left baseball after discovering golf, or rather embracing golf. The many hours he spent training meant that he could lower his handicap to that of the best 10% of all players in his region.

On December 30, 1975 in Cypress, California, the "child prodigy" Tiger Woods was born. And once again he was born to a passionate and domineering teacher. Earl and his second wife—who had no other children—decided to make little Tiger their number one priority. At just seven months old, Earl gave his son his first golf club and positioned Tiger on a special chair that allowed him to hit the ball without ever falling over. Little Tiger's training had begun! When the "child prodigy" joined the national American team at just nineteen years old, he had already been training hard for eighteen years and over thirty thousand hours! Time spent on deliberate practice, as Ericsson (2014) might have said.

So, does talent play no role at all then? That seems difficult to accept. When Dutch Formula 1 driver Max Verstappen recently became the youngest Grand Prix winner ever, everyone praised his unique gifts. Former Formula 1 world champion and racing legend Mario Andretti called Verstappen "a rare talent." Former racing driver Robert Doornbos said, "There is a certain aura around him." Might that be a family trait, since both his parents are racing drivers? Max Verstappen might be the next Mozart. Or Tiger Woods if you prefer. A young man that was trained to become an excellent racing driver by his father from a very young age. By the time he was seventeen—when many of us are still getting our drivers' licenses—little Max had already been deliberately practicing for fourteen years.

2.5 Winner DNA or Dedication?

As I see it, much of the confusion has come—and still comes—from the word "mainly." *Their performance is mainly a matter of having access to certain means.* Without talent, I figured, you cannot perform and continue performing. Talent is, therefore, a requirement for performance that can be positively affected by certain personality traits and the right fit with the environment.

Both Ericsson (2014, 2016) and myself (Kodden 2011, 2014) argue that, in addition to talent, the aspect of dedication and spending many hours doing something are most crucial when it comes to sustainable performance. But does that still apply to professionals today? Or are there perhaps other personality traits or performance criteria that might even be of much greater importance?

In 2012, Danish scientist Rasmus Ankersen published his book *The Gold Mine Effect*. Ankersen delved into the secrets of high performance and became the only expert to have actually lived amongst and trained with the best athletes in the world. *The Gold Mine Effect* (2012) was published in over 40 countries.

As a young soccer coach, Ankersen had once helped the Danish team FCMidtyll and set up Denmark's first soccer academy. His goal was simply to scout the best talents Denmark had to offer and then train them in order to transfer them to teams such as AC Milan, Inter, Barcelona et cetera for the highest fees possible. Most people felt that such a strategy was the only reason for a small team like FCMidtyll and to even exist.

Of all the talents Ankersen saw over the years as coach, one in particular stuck with him: Simon Kjaer. A not particularly talented soccer player who everyone had ignored, became the biggest success in the history of the team. How was it possible that Kjaer had gone unnoticed for so long? How many other Simon Kjaers might be out there? Ankersen couldn't get rid of the thought of so many talents simply going unnoticed. Was talent even the deciding factor?

2.6 Gold Mines

Rasmus Ankersen contemplated: "How is it possible, that a few small villages like Iten in Kenya and Bekoji in Ethiopia, keep delivering miracle runners? And why do Jamaicans always win the sprinting events at world championships and the Olympics? Why do 35% of the best female golfers in the world come from South Korea? How has Russia managed to produce 25% of the world's top 40 female tennis players in recent years? Why did most of the world's recent soccer greats come from Brazil?" Ankersen's quest for the answer to the question of what makes someone outperform anyone else in the world, led him to six, as he calls it, "goldmines" that produced one great after another.

In Kenya, Ethiopia, Jamaica (running), Russia (tennis), South Korea (golf), and Brazil (soccer), he spent six months training and trying to keep up with upcoming talents and established athletes.

If there was one thing that all of these goldmines had in common, Ankersen thought, it would be that they all provided an environment of practice and improvement. An environment where competitors serve to provide inspiration. "In Kenya, nobody runs alone, they do it together. Talents and the world's greats, running side by side." Just think of how inspiring that is. The person who wins the training run in Kenya on some Tuesday morning is likely to be the fastest person on the planet in that event. "Moreover, those talents see how hard their heroes have to work for their success. They see that the best in the world choose to continue training for another hour while the rest gives up. From a young age, they learn that the one who ends up winning is the one who wants it the most." Talent is good, character is better, it turned out. A conducive and inspiring environment appears to be crucial to fully developing talent.

Or as Ankersen puts it: "Talent exists, but it exists everywhere. It is about uncovering that talent." His most important conclusion and recommendation: "Not pushing your children to perform is the most irresponsible thing you can do as a parent. There is no DNA of a winner, the difference is made through dedication and practice!"

2.7 Deliberate Practice

Scientists from all over the world have been working for 150 years now to discover the secret of sustainable performance. Mountains of data are available from researchers who studied how top performers from, for instance, music, sports, and science, were able to do and achieve what they did. The general results of their studies, as well as those of my own, contradict what we have always thought. Namely, that talent and experience were the most important predictors for a sustainable, excellent performance. Talent does turn out to be a prerequisite—no talent, no performance— but talent and experience alone are wholly insufficient. As has been proven again and again, past performance is no guarantee for future results (Sengupta et al. 2008).

Still, many organizations value and use talent, experience, and past performance as the most important selection criteria when it comes to hiring, promoting, and rewarding their employees. Studies have indicated that the opposite is true. There is no evidence that experience is a reliable indicator for performance. On the contrary, in fact. Our knowledge about sustainable performance seems utterly inadequate (Kodden and Hupkes 2019; Kodden and Van Ingen 2019).

Anders Ericsson also concluded that it was not the quantity of practice that was important, but the quality. He made it his life's work to further study this quality of practice. Based on all the studies he had consulted, he came up with his theory of deliberate practice. It is not about practicing as much as you can, but about the quality of practice (Bandura 1977).

Deliberate practice means constantly confronting the limitations to your strongest aspects. Past performance should always be surpassed. It is not about just doing the bare minimum, it is about excelling. The Netherlands has too much of a culture of mediocrity, we practice all kinds of things and are not focused enough. Only when Daphne Schippers left combined events and specialized in sprint events, did she become a world-famous top athlete.

So much more can be said about talent and talent management. So many more books and studies can be quoted. Where to begin, where to end? That was my biggest challenge for this chapter. Eventually, I chose this one question: "To what extent is having talent truly important for sustainable performance?"

2.8   Results of the Study

In order to answer my main research question, I asked managers to answer two questions about the estimated talent of a random employee on a scale of one to five, varying from "completely agree" to "completely disagree."

This way, I charted the talent of over 1100 professionals and established the first variable related to the performance of these professionals.

My study on the importance of talent shows that having talent can only be considered conditionally important to performance. 'No performance without talent' is the tentative conclusion that can be drawn from the answers given by the supervisors and senior colleagues of over 1100 professionals. But in the end, the level of talent present showed very little significant correlation to performance. The aspect of talent ended up as number 9 on the list of all the performance criteria that had been suggested!

However, asked about the performance criterion they would use to hire new employees, the majority of CEOs said the following was the most important: The level of talent present for performing the job (see Appendix B: Most important results of the study on performance indicators). Asked how they considered or estimated this talent to be present in advance, most would say: "Well, based on diplomas, work experience, promotions, and the references they provided." In other words, based on past performance and the personal view that the talent deemed to be present in the candidate, would lead to further positive results in the future.

This was all wrong, which is not only demonstrated by my own study. For instance, a study by the University of Amsterdam together with temp agency Randstad from 2008 and a comprehensive international and longitudinal study by Schmidt and Hunter (1998) show that past performance as well as past references provide no guarantee at all for future results.

My study appears to fully confirm the theories by, among others, Billy Beane, Anders Ericsson, Daniel Pink, Malcolm Gladwell, Geoff Colvin, and Rasmus Ankersen: Talent is good, character is better! But which personal and character traits are to be considered crucial when it comes to sustainable performance? My quest continued.

References

Ankersen R (2012) The gold mine effect. Crack the secrets of high performance. Icon Books, London

Bandura A (1977) Self-efficacy: toward a unifying theory of behavioral change. Psychol Rev 84(2):191–215

Colvin G (2010) Talent is overrated. Penguin Group, New York, NY

Ericsson KA (ed) (2014) The road to excellence: the acquisition of expert performance in the arts and sciences, sports, and games. Psychology Press, New York, NY

Ericsson KA (2016) Peak: secrets from the new science of expertise. Houghton Mifflin Harcourt, Boston, MA

Galton F (2018) Hereditary character and talent. Suzeteo Publishers

Kodden SFGP (2011) Dedication. Nyenrode Business Universiteit

Kodden S (2014) Be a HERO. How to bring out leadership in everyone. Bernard Daniel Press

Kodden B, Hupkes L (2019) Organizational environment, personal resources and work engagement as predictors of coaching performance. J Manage Policy Pract 20(3)

Kodden SFGP, Van Ingen R (2019) Time for a new E/RA. J Appl Bus Econ

Meijers J (2016) Talent? Vooral hard blijven doorwerken. Consulted at https://fd.nl/morgen/1153168/talent-vooral-hard-blijven-doorwerken

Schmidt F, Hunter J (1998) The validity and utility of selection methods in personnel psychology: practical and Theoretical Implications of 85 years of research findings. Psychol Bull 124(2):262–274

Sengupta K, Abdel-Hamid TK, Van Wassenhove LN (2008) The experience trap. Harvard Bus Rev 86(2):94–101

Syed M (2011) Bounce: the myth of talent and the power of practice. Fourth Estate, London

Woods E (1997) Training a tiger. Harper Collins

Chapter 3
The Mediating Effect of Intelligence, Willpower, and Intrinsic Motivation on Talent and Performance

Abstract The number of studies on the positive symptoms of intrinsic work motivation appears to be located in the frequently demonstrated relationship between work engagement and performance. Work engagement is not only important to the individual employee, but also to the employer. Engaged and passionate employees are more productive, more customer-friendly, loyal to the organization, make fewer mistakes, and cause fewer accidents.

Keywords Intelligence · Willpower · Intrinsic motivation · Sustainable performance

3.1 Introduction

According to many studies, talent is overrated (Colvin 2010; Ericsson 2014, 2016; Syed 2011). The results of my study completely support this idea. Although to some degree talent seems a prerequisite for sustained performance, the actual influence of talent is minor. But then which personality traits are of vital importance for ensuring sustainable performance? How about intelligence? The mental giftedness and the ability to apply knowledge and experience in order to solve problems. Or perhaps willpower, as Baumeister and Tierney (2012) asserts in his book of the same title?

My second hypothesis is as follows:

Hypothesis 2
Having certain personality traits to a greater or a lesser degree positively or negatively influences the relationship between talent and performance (Fig. 3.1).

3.2 Intelligence and Willpower

Swedish professor and psychologist Anders Ericsson concludes that in addition to talent, the amount of deliberate practice is vitally important to sustainable performance. But what about willpower and intelligence?

© The Author(s) 2020
B. Kodden, *The Art of Sustainable Performance*, SpringerBriefs in Business,
https://doi.org/10.1007/978-3-030-46463-9_3

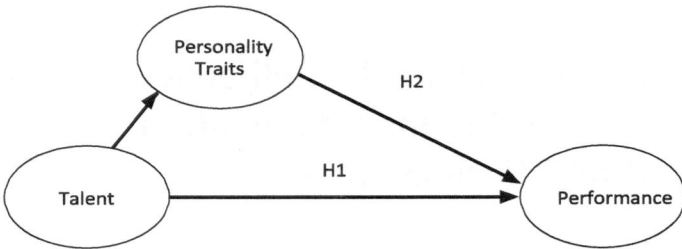

Fig. 3.1 Hypothesis 2

In 2014 and, more recently, 2016, Anders Ericsson's studies and research received criticism (Macnamara et al. 2016). Despite thorough analyses of thousands of studies on top performers showing the importance of deliberate practice, other researchers concluded that different phenomena played a greater role in sustainable performance. For example, the deliberate practice was an important factor, but not the sole explanation for sustainable performance, studies by Roy Baumeister, and John Tierney showed.

Roy Baumeister is one of the most important psychologists of our time. He is a professor of psychology at Florida State University and professor by special appointment at the Vrije Universiteit Amsterdam. He started his career as a social psychologist researching self-esteem and self-confidence in the seventies. Along the way, he discovered that self-confidence was not the be-all and end-all that people thought it was. He started exploring other concepts such as self-regulation, self-control, and willpower. Whereas Freudians see human behavior as the result of mostly subconscious processes, Baumeister for years has emphasized the importance of conscious control of one's behavior. His most recent book, *Willpower*, which he wrote together with science journalist John Tierney of *The New York Times*, is about the importance of willpower and self-control and how you can improve the two.

According to Baumeister and Tierney, when you look at the personality traits that are important to achieve success in life, it all comes down to two traits: intelligence and willpower. To them, success in life refers to "being happy, healthy, living longer, having less mental health problems, less physical ailments, better relations with other people, being more successful, and thus less likely to commit crimes and end up in jail." As it turns out, good self-control has a positive influence on all those things. According to Baumeister, "you could even argue that self-control plays a role in many of the societal problems of our time, such as financial issues (like the 2008 financial crisis), violence, obesity, alcohol, and drug abuse".

In the introduction to their book *Willpower* (2012), Baumeister and Tierney describes how initially, they were just as skeptical about willpower as most people in their field. Willpower was a nineteenth-century concept; Victorian ideas, strict and antiquated. In the twentieth century, it was generally assumed that self-esteem and self-confidence were much more important factors to success.

3.3 Discipline and Rules

In their book, Baumeister and Tierney argue that the average member of our modern society has far less willpower—the will to persevere—than people used to have. "That is partly due to the fact that schools and parents do not think discipline is important anymore. This is also the result of the self-esteem movement of the seventies, which emphasized how important it is to praise and encourage your children. Since that time, concepts such as punishing, disciplining, and criticizing have become increasingly unpopular. This is not a positive development, nor for self-confidence. It doesn't help any child to be constantly praised. Children often do not receive any clue as to why exactly they are being praised. If you really want to teach your child to be self-confident, you should make clear what the rules are. Subsequently, you should tell them that they behave well when they follow the rules, and badly when they break them. That way the child will learn that his or her actions have consequences."

3.4 Ego Depletion

Baumeister compares willpower to a muscle. If you use it too much, it will tire out. "Think of a normal workday. All-day you were looking forward to telling your smug boss what you really think of him. However, you maintained control over yourself and even greeted him in a friendly fashion. Then you arrive home. Your partner asks you if you remembered to get groceries, as you had promised. Suddenly you feel a blind rage building up inside you and you end up screaming and cursing."

A typical example of the phenomena for which Baumeister coined the term "ego depletion": running out of willpower. Ego depletion refers to a person's reduced ability to regulate their behavior. "Everyone has a limited amount of willpower per day," explains Baumeister. "And we use that willpower for a variety of unrelated tasks, but which share a connection through this one energy source. If someone focuses on not eating too much all day, he or she might erupt into a classic example of road rage later. Nevertheless, you can always improve your self-control, simply by training it."

In my study, willpower, self-control, and self-confidence were also suggested as (potentially) important elements of personality traits that indicate sustainable performance. For my study, I used the following definition of willpower: the will to persevere and the ability to control yourself. Self-control is defined as the ability to control your whims and impulses. Not performing action now because it conflicts with what you want to achieve in the long term. And then there's also self-confidence: the belief that someone can successfully control and influence his or her surroundings.

3.5 Intrinsic Motivation

And what about intrinsic motivation? As I said at the start and as others (Colvin 2010; Syed 2011, for instance) have said before; talent is overrated. But what is the role of intrinsic motivation in sustainable performance?

Intrinsic and extrinsic motivation are two different sources of motivation that are often distinguished from each other. The theoretical boundaries between these two concepts are not always clear, though. According to the self-determination theory, extrinsic motives are motives that originate from external sources. For instance, the promise of a reward or penalty for a specific action. On the other hand, intrinsic motives come from the person him/herself. These are not about getting an external reward or avoiding a penalty, but about the intrinsic value of the activity itself or a future goal.

As a metaphor; intrinsic motivation is about the game, extrinsic motivation about the rewards. In this study, I considered intrinsic motivation to be enjoying your job and having fun while doing it. Extrinsic motivation I understood as having a certain standard of living, making a lot of money, working for a paycheck. Both definitions are similar to those of Gagné and Deci (2005) and Gagné et al. (2010).

Several scientific studies indicate differences between behavior that arises from extrinsic motivation and behavior that is motivated intrinsically. According to scientific studies, people intrinsically motivated to perform a specific action demonstrate:

- a higher level of concentration;
- more creativity. This is in part due to a higher level of concentration, a higher willingness to take risks, being more playful and having more flexible trains of thought;
- increased feelings of self-competence and pride;
- increased enjoyment while performing their task.

Studies further show that extrinsic motivation can move non-intrinsically motivated people into action (Pink 2009). The downside, however, is that the prospect of a reward or penalty will need to continue to exist, or the extrinsic motivation will stop having any effect at all. Intrinsic motivation, on the other hand, can occur independently from external factors and can, therefore, be seen as more sustainable.

3.6 The Motivation Continuum

The motivation theory, or Self-Determination Theory (SDT), by Deci and Ryan has continued to develop since the 1970s. An important early milestone was the publication of *Intrinsic Motivation and Self-determination in Human Behavior* in 1985 (Deci and Ryan 1985). Years later, in 2000, Ryan and Deci published "Intrinsic and

Extrinsic Motivations: Classic Definitions and New Directions", which is still considered one of the leading review articles in the field. In it, they offer insights into different forms and levels of motivation, and the mechanisms through which an organization's environment can contribute to the motivation of its employees. Whereas motivation used to be considered a unidimensional concept, which people possessed to a greater or lesser degree, Deci and Ryan show that the concept of "motivation" is much more complex and multidimensional. In the previously mentioned publication from the year 2000, Ryan and Deci presented a "taxonomy of human motivation."

In other words, a-motivation continuum. Their continuum starts on the left with a-motivation (absence of intention) and then moves to the right through four degrees of extrinsic motivation, ending with the most powerful form of motivation: intrinsic motivation.

Deci and Ryan also posited that intrinsic motivation is not a fixed thing, but rather a snapshot: An employee might be intrinsically motivated when starting a new job, but subsequently lose his/her intrinsic motivation for a variety of reasons (Fig. 3.2).

No motivation   **Strong motivation**

Motivation-type	A-motivation	Extrinsic motivation				Intrinsic motivation
		External regulation	Introjection	Identifi-cation	Integration	
Related processes	Experienced low com-petence level, absence of intentions	Aimed at external rewards Compliant, reactive	Ego plays an important role Aimed at- validation from others	Consciously appreciating certain behavior See the value	In accordance with own values and standards	Interest Enjoyment Satisfaction from activity
Level of autonomy	Absent	Very low	Low	Some level of autonomy	Significant level of autonomy	Significant level of autonomy

Fig. 3.2 Deci and Ryan' motivation continuum (Deci and Ryan 1985)

3.7   Motivation 3.0

Pink (2009) demonstrates that several theories have been formed in recent decades about where people get their drive from. In his book *Drive* (2011), Pink links Deci and Ryan's motivation study (2000) to Csikszentmihalyi's study on flow (Csikszentmihalyi 1975, 2007).

Motivation 1.0 describes people's basic need to survive as their main drive. Motivation 2.0 includes managing employees using positive and negative reinforcement. Motivation 3.0 assumes the paradigm that people find their drive when they are intrinsically motivated. In his book, Pink explains why Motivation 2.0 is outdated and how you can use Motivation 3.0 to motivate people. According to Pink, three elements are essential to stimulate, realize, and retain motivation 3.0:

1. *Autonomy.* People should always have autonomy when it comes to their tasks, time, group, and work methods says Pink.
2. *Mastery.* Engagement van only is achieved through mastery. It is important that the work that you have to perform is in line with your talents. According to Pink, mastery is, therefore, a mindset. As it can always be improved, true mastery is essentially unattainable. That's why the entire concept of mastery results in people striving for it, stimulating to pursue mastery. It offers intrinsic motivation.
3. *Meaning.* According to Pink, the first two elements are essential. However, a third element is required for a proper balance. This element is meaning, something that provides a context for the other two. Autonomous people who strive for mastery, perform at a very high level. But the ones who do so with a sense of a higher purpose can achieve even more.

In his book *Drive* (2009), Pink points out the importance of intrinsic motivation by referring to several scientific studies. But like Deci and Ryan, he also argues that intrinsic motivation is not fixed. He believes it can fluctuate depending on how much autonomy someone has been given, how they are stimulated to strive for mastery and have a purpose, meaning.

It reminded me again of the story of Billy Bean and his will to get to the core of performance. After reading all, the aforementioned research and studies, I was as curious as ever: to what extent are willpower, self-control, self-confidence, intelligence, intrinsic and/or extrinsic motivation truly important for sustainable performance?

3.8   Results of the Study

This study demonstrates that intelligence and intrinsic motivation are in fact very important for sustainable performance. Intrinsic motivation turned out to be the fourth most important predictor of sustainable performance. Intelligence was number five. And just as important: a large-scale research project by researchers from the University of Amsterdam also shows intelligence tests to be one of the best predictors of future performance (UvA 2008).

The personal trait of willpower, on the other hand, did not show an important relation to performance. It did not even make the top 10 of the most important performance criteria. Unlike the variable dedication (one of the three elements of work engagement), which was the sixth-best predictor of performance. This concept also seems closely related to performance predictor number four, intrinsic motivation.

Willpower seems to have more of the characteristics of extrinsic motivation, and dedication seems more closely related to intrinsic motivation to perform our jobs. "I, or rather, we have a goal and I am dedicated to achieving it." Instead of, "I have to do something and for that I need willpower." Another explanation for the fact that willpower is not an important predictor for performance might lie in the fact that my research was done in a corporate environment—performing as a professional—whereas the studies by Baumeister and Tierney were more focused on people's personal lives—performing as private persons. In the latter context, the role of willpower seems to be much more significant. After all, self-control and managing and controlling your own behavior are crucial factors in resisting all of modern life's temptations, as the studies by Baumeister and Tierney show time and again (Baumeister and Tierney 2012).

Another remarkable outcome of my study is a reasonably strong, significant correlation between extrinsic motivation and sustainable performance. Extrinsic motivation did not turn out to be one of the most important predictors but still managed to take 10th place, after talent. And if you only look at one particular element of performance, namely the speed of achievements, then the importance of extrinsic motivation increases significantly, becoming a very important predictor, in fact (number 3). Extrinsically motivated professionals seem to deliver quick and short-term performance but lose their drive after a while when other factors are no longer in effect. This matches Daniel Pink's theory (2009).

When asked what performance criterion they would use to hire new employees, most CEOs put the amount of talent present for doing the job at the top of the list. Intrinsic motivation came in second. Number 3 was intelligence. Willpower landed at number 7 (for more information, see Appendix B: Most important results of the study on performance indicators).

To the question of how these CEOs would determine the presence of intrinsic motivation, intelligence, and willpower during or after interviews, most could not give a clear answer. "Well, that's a good question," was a common response. Only a few mentioned that they started with an intelligence test, but almost all indicated that interviews and their own opinion determined whether or not they would hire someone. As Steve Jobs put it, "So, in the end, it's ultimately based on your gut."

This study has shown that professionals who deliver sustainable performance are intelligent, dedicated, and intrinsically motivated individuals. However, the two most important predictors for performance turn out to be two different traits: adaptability and self-efficacy!

References

Baumeister RF and Tierney J (2012) Willpower. Why self-control is the secret to success. Penquin Books New York

Colvin G (2010) Talent is overrated. Penguin Group, New York, NY

Csikszentmihalyi M (1975) Beyond boredom and anxiety. Jossey-Bass Publishers, San Francisco, CA

Csikszentmihalyi M (2007) Flow Psychologie van de optimale ervaring. Boom, Amsterdam

Deci EL, Ryan RM (1985) Intrinsic motivation and self-determination in human behavior. Plenum, New York, NY

Deci EL, Ryan RM (2000) The 'what' and' why' of goal pursuits: human needs and the self-determination of behavior. Psychol Inq 11(4):227–268

Ericsson KA (ed) (2014) The road to excellence: the acquisition of expert performance in the arts and sciences, sports, and games. Psychology Press, New York, NY

Ericsson KA (2016) Peak: secrets from the new science of expertise. Houghton Mifflin Harcourt, Boston, MA

Gagné M, Deci EL (2005) Self-determination theory and work motivation. J Organ Behav 26(4):331–362

Gagné M, Forest J, Vansteenkiste M, Crevier-Braud L, Van den Broeck A, Aspeli AK et al (2010) Validation evidence in ten languages for the revised motivation at work scale. Concordia University, Montreal

Macnamara B, Moreau D, Hambrick DZ (2016) The relationship between deliberate practice and performance in sports. Meta-Anal Perspect Psychol Sci 11(3):333–350

Pink D (2009) The surprising truth about what motivates us. Riverhead Books

Syed M (2011) Bounce: the myth of talent and the power of practice. Fourth Estate, London

UvA (2008) Personeelsselectie in tijden van krapte. Onderzoek door UvA en Randstad. Diemen

Chapter 4
The Ability to Adapt

Abstract The competence to adapt to a fast-changing environment influences sustainable outcomes. Adaptability refers to "an individual's ability, skill, disposition, willingness, and/or motivation to change or fit the different task, social, or environmental features." Adaptability is considered by many researchers to be a key source of mental resources. Mental resources are especially important for new employees who are facing a totally new environment. The increasingly changing nature of modern organizations requires employees to constantly improve their ability to adapt.

Keywords Adaptability · Agile talent · Personal traits · Sustainable performance

4.1 Introduction

Our world is getting smaller and smaller, increasingly more digital, and undergoing constant change. Technological advancements follow one another ever more rapidly and the life cycles of organizations and teams are getting shorter. We can all sense it; what is considered new and successful today, might be obsolete tomorrow.

In a changing world, the only constant is change itself. This seems particularly true for organizations. Growing markets, expanding businesses, stronger competition, privatization, deregulation, mergers, and the rise of network organizations and new technologies have made change management a fact of life for our organizations. Large, new (job) markets are emerging and new technologies have thrown existing business models out of the window (Aguirre and Alpern 2014). Nevertheless, so far no research has shown that change processes have become any more successful than they were twenty years ago (Cozijnsen and Vrakking 2013). Instead, the opposite might be true. Several studies show that over 50%—some would argue over 70%—of planned organizational changes end prematurely or fail eventually (Kotter 1995; Hammer 1996; Beer and Nohria 2000; Burnes 2004; Kodden and Van Ingen 2019).

B. Kodden, *The Art of Sustainable Performance*, SpringerBriefs in Business,
https://doi.org/10.1007/978-3-030-46463-9_4

4.2   The Importance of Adaptability

The speed with which organizations have to adapt is increasing exponentially. On average, they also do not survive as long as they used to. In his book, *Serial Innovators: Firms that change the world,* Claudio Feser states that the average life cycle of American businesses today is only fifteen years. In the mid-twentieth century, the average was forty-five years. If this trend continues, the life cycle might be down to only five or ten years in the near future (Knegtmans 2016). Adaptability is key if organizations and teams want to survive.

Adaptability is not just something old and well-established organizations struggle with. Start-ups, young businesses, and mature organizations also deal with it. It is all about adaptability. Or more specifically; it *continues to be* all about adaptability. After all, change has always been around. What is different today though is the speed at which change is taking place, mostly as a result of information technology. Furthermore, these technological changes are not linear, but rather exponential. Moore's Law states that the processing power of computer chips doubles every two years. In order to remain successful, we have to adapt to exponential growth instead of linear growth. That has significant consequences and applications. The world's fastest-growing media company (Facebook) does not own any content, the world's largest taxi company (Uber) does not own any cars, the world's largest retail business (Alibaba) has no stock and the world's largest provider of short-term lodging (Airbnb) does not have any real estate. New start-ups are emerging ever more quickly and through innovative use of information technology, manage to conquer a major market share in very little time. Of course, this exponential growth also has downsides, one being the failure of many competitors that are not able to adapt.

4.3   Vuca

A popular acronym in the US is "VUCA," which is also becoming more common in the Netherlands. The four letters stand for:

- *volatile* (rapidly changing);
- *uncertain* (unpredictable);
- *complex* (complexity);
- *ambiguous* (haziness of reality).

VUCA is the rapidly changing world we now live in as individuals and as organizations. A world that is defined by a high level of uncertainty and complexity. VUCA also shows the importance of adaptability now that it is becoming increasingly difficult to create detailed plans for five or ten year periods. All aspects are changing more and more rapidly and small factors can have increasingly significant and complex consequences. That is why both as individuals and as organizations, we need to be more flexible and sustain that flexibility. That way one can quickly and easily adapt in ways that have a positive effect on the most important stakeholders (Knegtmans 2016).

4.4 Radical Changes

Consider the developments in organizations such as Nokia and Kodak. Although Nokia managed to reinvent itself several times and transformed from a wood pulp manufacturer into a rubber manufacturer and then into a producer of personal computers and mobile phones, the company failed to make one crucial step. Despite the fact that the Finnish phone giant had a record year in 2007 and had been the market leader for a long time, a lack of innovation brought the company to the brink of ruin. It waited too long to switch to a new operating system, allowing Apple and Google to quickly overtake the Finns. Despite its long history of change, innovating too slowly led to the marginalization of this once renowned global brand in only a few years (Knegtmans 2016).

Tribes
Many organizations are currently working to become as agile as possible, for instance by structuring themselves as tribes. Agile organizations work with different squads; small multi-disciplinary teams of no more than nine people. All these squads have their own objectives and they bear the responsibility to achieve them. In a squad, colleagues from all disciplines are required to achieve the objective work together to succeed. Once the assignment has been completed, the squad is dissolved and the members are assigned to different squads.

New ways of organizing such as agile management and working in tribes—approaches that we recognize from companies such as Spotify, Netflix, Google, and ING—are radical and revolutionary for many organizations. But many studies have shown that changes to organizational structures and methods are in no way a guarantee for success (Kotter 1995; Hammer 1996; Beer and Nohria 2000; Burnes 2004; Kodden and Van Ingen 2019). In the end, it always comes down to employees that may or may not be able to function in the new structure and work method. After all, not everyone is equally adaptable to change. Successful change management in organizations mainly depends on the adaptability of its professionals.

4.5 Agile Talent

According to a 2016 report by the World Economic Forum, 35% of skills that are currently crucial to professionals will change significantly within the next five years. *Harvard Business Review* says that 70% of current top performers lack the qualities necessary for their future roles (Martin and Schmidt 2010).

An important new requirement for sustainable performance, according to Ralf Knegtmans (author of the book *Agile Talent),* is therefore the ability of business to respond to technological developments as well as being able to attract and recruit future, or agile, talent. Knegtmans defines agile talent as talent that is able to adapt quickly to new circumstances and in doing so, is able to stay future-proof. These professionals are innovative and eager to learn and renew a business from within. "Only by using this talent, can businesses themselves become more agile," explains Knegtmans (2016). Agile companies exist by the grace of talent. Because the world is changing so quickly, organizations also need different people, according to Knegtmans. "That means that we need to have different selection criteria."

Higher education will also need to respond to this changing need. After all, knowledge expires quickly. We are currently training people for jobs that we know will not be around much longer. In that sense, higher education still seems to be structured like a nineteenth-century factory that puts students on a conveyor belt curriculum. "Drop-outrates are 35% and the ones that do make it, end up with a diploma if we continue like that, we will never be able to make life-long learning a reality," says Henk Hagoort, chairman of the board for Windesheim University of Applied Sciences. Financial economics professor Sylvester Eijffinger, who in his role as chairman of Tilburg University Society advises the university board about renewing the curricula says, "We must realize that the roles we are currently training people for, will no longer be relevant for the job market in five or ten years. We should be training competences, not jobs" (Het Financieel Dagblad 2017).

I wondered how important a professional's adaptability currently is for their own performance and that of their organization. As I was asking myself, I considered that it may actually be a rhetorical question…

4.6 Results of the Study

For this study, adaptability was defined as the willingness (to change) and the ability of a person to adapt to a changing environment, work methods, work hours, tasks, responsibilities, and behavior by others. Willingness to change was defined similarly to Cozijnsen and Vrakking (2013): A positive behavioral intent by an employee regarding the introduction of changes in the organizational or departmental structure, culture, or work method, resulting in an effort by the employee to support or even speed up the change process.

The adaptability of professionals is indeed the main factor for sustainable performance, as shown by this study as well. As it turns out, adaptability is vitally important for personal and team performance. With the exception of self-efficacy (Chap. 5), it is even the most important factor!

Research and studies (Strauss et al. 2015) show that adaptability is a personal trait that is very difficult to learn in a course or training seminar. Some professionals are more resistant to change because they experience inconsistency. Things are not going as they expected. And if those changes are then also imposed on them by others, for instance, through a reoreferrganization, this may lead to stress, uncertainty, and lack of productivity. Some people are (much) more adaptable than others, studies show.

As Roy Baumeister also concluded with regards to willpower, adaptability can be trained to a certain extent, but will also simply snap at some point. How soon depends on the person.

The trick for managers in rapidly organizations, therefore, appears to be more than just creating support for methods like Agile and Scrum, or sending employees to courses and training seminars related to those methods. They also need to select employees who have this important personal trait. After all, the agility of an organization is largely determined by the agility of its people (Knegtmans 2016).

The Dutch CEOs I approached, however, did not pay a lot of attention to adaptability as a selection criterion and put it in a dismal 11th place on the list of personality traits they use to hire professionals. A surprising, perhaps even shocking result considering the importance of adaptability for an organization's survival, and considering the fact that adaptability is a trait that is difficult to improve.

References

Aguirre D, Alpern M (2014) 10 belangrijkste punten voor verander management. Manage Executive 5:12–13

Beer M, Nohria N (2000) Cracking the code of change. Harvard Bus Rev 78(2):133–141

Burnes B (2004) Managing change, 4th edn. Financial Times/Prentice Hall, Harlow

Cozijnsen AJ, Vrakking WJ (2013) Basisboek Veranderkunde. Kluwer, Deventer

Het Financieel Dagblad (2017). Hoger Onderwijs moet radicaal hervormen. https://fd.nl/economie-politiek/1192934/hoger-onderwijs-moet-radicaal-hervormen

Hammer M (1996) Beyond reengineering: how the process-centered organization is changing our lives. Harper Business, New York, NY

Knegtmans R (2016) Agile talent. Negen cruciale stappen bij de selectie van het toptalent van morgen. Business Contact, Amsterdam

Kodden SFGP, Van Ingen R (2019) Time for a new E/RA. J Appl Bus Econ

Kotter JP (1995) Leading change: why transformation efforts fail. Harvard Bus Rev 73(2):59–67

Martin J and Schmidt C (2010) How to keep your top talent. Harvard Bus Rev 5

Strauss K, Griffin MA, Parker SK (2015) Building and sustaining proactive behaviors: the role of adaptivity and job satisfaction. J Bus Psychol 30(1):63–72

Chapter 5
The Impact of Self-efficacy

Abstract Based on studies, the degree of self-efficacy appears to have a strong relationship with positive indicators of employees, such as their well-being, work engagement, and achievements. Other positive indicators of self-efficacy have also been observed, such as the positive effects on well-being and negative effects on burnout. Self-efficacy was described by the originator of the concept, Bandura, as the belief in one's own ability to complete a particular task in a particular situation. It concerns the belief in one's own ability and not the possession of specific competences.

Keywords Self-efficacy · Personality traits · Work engagement · Sustainable performance

5.1 Introduction

"The best performers are the ones who continue on paths that match their strengths and talents and that show their self-efficacy and originality," says Adam Grant in his book *Originals* (2016). Adam Grant (1981) is a professor at Wharton and a lauded researcher in the field of management and phycology. He earned his degree at Harvard with honors and was awarded with the John Howard Scholarship for his research. He has been named one of the 440 best psychologists in the world.

For 14 years, Adam Grant studied five thousand entrepreneurs and discovered that the most successful of them only followed a handful of rules. The five most important are as follows:

1. Continue to wonder what has not been done yet, or at least not in a certain way, and ask yourself why.
2. Become an idea machine; keep active and keep developing.
3. Be aware of your weaknesses and learn to use them as little as possible.
4. Use your strengths to become increasingly experienced in what you specialize in.
5. Always keep your goal—your reason—in mind!

B. Kodden, *The Art of Sustainable Performance*, SpringerBriefs in Business,
https://doi.org/10.1007/978-3-030-46463-9_5

Adam Grant's outcomes seem to perfectly match those uncovered by Ericsson and others in their studies: deliberate practice is vital for sustainable performance. Keep doing and repeating those things that match your passion and strengths, and make conscious choices in how you use your time and energy to go from good to excellent. And always remember that it is about courage. Failure is part of the deal.

5.2   Risk Avoidance

"Regretting something that you have not done, is worse than regretting something you did do. I can accept failure," as basketball legend Michael Jordan put it. "Everyone fails at something. But I can't accept not trying. I have missed at least 9000 shots in my life, lost over 300 games, and 26 times I was entrusted with the deciding shot and missed. I failed many times in my life. And that's why I was successful."

Despite popular belief, successful entrepreneurs, as well as legendary athletes, top musicians, scientists, and others who excel at what they do, are not actually risk-takers, says Grant. According to Grant, the word "entrepreneur" literally means "avoiding risks." After fourteen years of research, he concluded that the one thing successful entrepreneurs have in common is that they strive for originality while keeping all other factors as stable and secure as possible. That way they can be self-effective in the areas where their strengths lie.

Take the "rebel" Steve Jobs for instance. He only quit his job and school after he had been developing his software ideas for years. Larry Page, creator and founder of Google, continued his studies at Stanford for years before actually starting his own business and dedicating all his time and energy to it. Henry Ford's story is quite similar too. He continued working for Thomas Edison for two years before he felt ready to quit his job. Subconsciously, these men all felt that they first needed to further develop their ideas - they had to get more relevant experience - before they could put everything aside in order to deliver their unique performance (Grant 2016). Practice makes perfect, is something Adam Grant also concludes.

5.3   Domain-Specific Knowledge Is Power

How is it possible that IBM s world-famous Deep Blue, which can analyze 200 million moves per second, can still lose chess games against grandmasters? The answer lies in the fact that people have access to knowledge that computers cannot comprehend. This has been called "deep knowledge" by computer scientists such as Cohen and Feigenbaum (Cohen and Feigenbaum 2014). The most important ingredient in any expert system is knowledge.

But as is the case with experience, not all knowledge is equal. It is about domain-specific knowledge. As Geoff Colvin puts it: "Power is having the right knowledge."

Dutch psychologist, Adriaan de Groot, studied the ways in which the knowledge of world-class chess players differed from that of average players. Surprisingly, top performers did not seem to consider more moves than average players. Nor were they able to see many more moves ahead.

But then what was the difference? It turned out that world-class players had much greater specific knowledge about chess than average players. Up to a hundred times more even. Moreover, they were able to better organize that knowledge, making it easier for them to access it. That is how they were able to come up with fundamentally different solutions compared to average players.

The opposite is true for many businesses. A lot of averagely performing companies give their employees—particularly upcoming managers—the opportunity to work in many positions in the company in order to learn every aspect of the business. It is the top-performing organizations that let their leaders work in the same domain for long periods of time. Because of this, they know everything there is to know about their field of expertise and network. The most successful companies, therefore, train their managers in a domain-specific way (Harvard Business Review, June 2006). The most successful leaders are the ones who have this "deeper" knowledge. Deliberate practice and self-efficacy are what make the difference. Deliberate practice enables you to build specific knowledge and skills that you need to achieve sustainable performance in your area of expertise.

By continually challenging yourself and improving your strengths, you shape an attitude that can later be labeled as unconscious competence. Without even being aware of it, you collect more knowledge and information than others around you. As a result, you require less insight than others at certain critical moments (p. 87). You're able to respond appropriately without any help.

Think about it for a second; what good is all that knowledge if you are not able to access it at the moment supreme, in just a fraction of a second? Sustainable performance seems to require skill related to your strengths. That is the skill you should consciously train in order to feel confident enough to trust in it.

5.4 What Is Self-efficacy?

What exactly is self-efficacy? According to the creator of the Self-Efficacy Theory, Albert Bandura, self-efficacy is the confidence that a person has in their own ability to successfully influence their surroundings by completing a certain task or solving a problem (Bandura 1977). Self-efficacy is considered one of the most important elements in theories on motivation. People are more likely to be motivated to perform a certain action when they feel they have the ability to do it successfully. According to Albert Bandura, they are more likely to display and continue the desired behavior. Self-efficacy influences many areas, including motivation for study and career choice.

Self-efficacy differs from self-confidence in that the latter is about confidence in yourself, whereas self-efficacy is the estimated ability one has to complete a certain task. It is different from the concept of "efficiency" because it is not about a person's actual efficiency, but about how much confidence they have in their efficiency.

When people with high self-efficacy achieve a certain goal, there is a good chance that their next goal will be more challenging. At least, according to theory. And if a goal is not achieved, the way people react varies from person to person. Some respond with renewed commitment, others with despair, and apathy. Self-efficacy is an important factor in this. Results can be self-reinforcing. If a person is not successful at achieving a new goal, it can reduce their self-efficacy, making it even less likely that they will achieve a subsequent goal because their motivation was lowered. On the other hand, successfully achieving goals can increase self-efficacy and therefore the future likelihood of success.

5.5   Deliberate Practice and Self-efficacy

But how can deliberate practice effectively be put into practice with regard to self-efficacy? Several studies show that by continually repeating the right exercises and putting them into practice, an average professional can transform into an exceptional performer (Bandura 1977; Collins 2001; Colvin 2010; Kodden 2014). It is the companies and individuals that know what is required to take little steps every day towards continual improvement that manages to achieve unique performance. Starting small and moving onto large, going from an A to an A+ , it requires deliberate practice and self-efficacy.

According to Colvin, it can be argued that generally speaking, practice is simply the idea of constantly pushing yourself. Deliberate practice refers to a level of practice that goes beyond that of what normal people do (Colvin 2010). More specifically: constantly practicing your strengths, allows you to yield larger returns, know more, and remember more. According to Colvin, years of deliberate practice can even change an individual's body and mind. Let us take a closer look at these three aspects.

5.6   Top Performers See Less and Understand More

As a result of deliberate practice, top performers receive more relevant information. In his book, *Blink: The power of thinking without thinking* (2005), best-selling author Malcolm Gladwell describes how certain top athletes have the ability to achieve incredible response times. Tennis players who could anticipate the direction of their opponent's serve before they even made it. Top players who had gone beyond normal practice and were no longer focusing on reflexes and response times—limited by the laws of the universe—or on the ball itself, which would simply go too fast when served by the world's top servers, but instead on their opponent's body language. Researches proved that the eyes of these "deliberate practitioners" were no longer focused on the ball at the moment of the serve, but rather on the hip, shoulders, and arms of the person serving. By "letting go" of the ball, they managed to predict its direction and were able to react in time to balls that would normally be moving too fast for natural human reflexes and would have been impossible to return.

Other researchers presented a movie clip to both a group of average tennis players and a group of top players that showed hundreds of serves. Both groups were asked to predict the direction in which the ball would be played. The group of average players had no clue, but the best players could make accurate predictions, allowing them to return the serve. They were able to react quicker without improving their reflexes. They knew where the ball was going.

This phenomenon of seeing less and understanding more can be found in many studies. Not just in sports, but many other activities as well. In his book *Talent is Overrated* (2010), Colvin takes the activity of typing as an example. The fastest typists are able to type at a certain speed because they are able to stay ahead in the text instead of looking at their fingers to produce text that they are working on at that moment. The same is true for juggling. The best jugglers do not look at the balls, but at the paths that the balls will follow. As soon as the path changes as a result of a mistake, they compensate. That way they can juggle a lot more balls or pins than others. By seeing less, they actually see more!

Another example is a hospital study. It studied how x-rays were interpreted by radiologists. Although the response time is not as important in this case, the correct interpretation definitely is. Both expert radiologists as well as first and fourth-year students were asked to correctly evaluate the x-rays. They were told that time was not a factor.

The correct evaluation was paramount. The x-ray examples that were used displayed several serious ailments, such as tumors or a collapsed lung.

It should come as no surprise that the expert group had the best results in the study. When it came to evaluating the x-rays, domain-specific experts seemed better able to interpret the smallest details. Their eyesight was not demonstrably better than the other groups, but they could still interpret the details better and combine them into an evaluation that was not obvious at first glance.

The same thing happened in a study on pilots and musicians. Practiced participants turned out to be able to look beyond the surface. Top performers see less, which makes them perceive more. They also understand the importance of indicators that average performers do not notice. Sometimes the indicators are obvious, other times they are not. Take Laura Ritten house, for instance. A financial analyst, she showed that the more times an annual performance report had the word "I" in it, the worse a company would perform in the future. In other words, *egomaniacs are bad news*. Finding these kinds of—not always obvious—indicators requires extensive practice and experience.

5.7 Top Performers See the Future

Top professionals know more because they often literally see the future. Top musicians stay ahead of their song texts and the best typists manage a similar feat. The power of looking ahead lies in gaining a new perspective in addition to the ones already available. This extra perspective is the difference between average and exceptional performance. Steve Jobs already knew where he was going before he invented his new products or had others do it for him. It was not about the product, but what the product would make possible. Although the product did not even exist yet, Steve Jobs had already thought of a use for it.

Practice makes perfect, that's what makes Steve Jobs a true inspiration to me. His biggest strength was the additional perspective he had developed after years of deliberate practice. The same was true for Wolfgang Amadeus Mozart, Tiger Woods, the Hungarian Polgar sisters, and now the Netherlands' own Max Verstappen. Years of deliberate practice gave them the additional perspective that allowed them to see into the future and produce incredible musical compositions, golf swings, chess moves, and lap times.

5.8 Top Performers Know More by Seeing Less

The aspect of knowing more by seeing less turns out to be vital for success in every domain of our lives. Because we are never able to receive and process as much information as we want in order to make a correct assessment, it is important to make the right decision in as little time as possible. Regardless of whether it is about ER surgeons, police officers responding to emergencies or professional athletes that have to react within a fraction of a second; the ability to respond quickly and correctly is a definite competitive advantage. The underlying skill is unconscious competence (Chap. 10) to evaluate the right indicators for success at specific moments in time. Top performers intuitively know how to distinguish the relevant aspects. And, as it turns out, this skill requires deliberate practice.

5.9 A Powerful Combination

Self-efficacy combined with deliberate practice as a source of constant change, and as the most powerful energy source for sustainable performance; exactly how powerful this combination is, has been demonstrated by research into the physical changes of sustainably performing professionals. Experienced and high-level endurance athletes were shown to have a larger than the average heart. A characteristic that was previously considered a natural competitive advantage—like talent—but later turned out to be the result of intense training. When these professionals stopped training, their hearts would return to normal size. Top athletes did not only change the size of their heart, but also its composition (the amount of fast-twitch muscle fibers versus slow ones).

It turns out that even our brains can change the composition. An example is children who start practicing music. Their brains start to change; the regions that develop finger control, start to take up noticeably more space than in children who do not play an instrument. A study of London cab drivers also shows that drivers who had practiced for two years had developed their brains in a way that showed an increase in size of the area associated with spatial awareness and navigation. How is that possible? According to research, it is mostly the result of a bodily substance known as myelin. This is a white substance that improves the functioning of nerve fibers and neurons (Colvin 2010).

Myelin

Myelin is a fleshy substance that surrounds a lot of the axons in our nervous systems. Myelin gives the substance its white color. It allows impulses to be sent more quickly (increasing from 2 m/s to a maximum of 120 m/s). Without myelin, those impulses would take much longer to move from one nerve cell to the next through the axon. This is particularly important in the case of longer distances (such as in the peripheral nervous system). The myelin sheet consists of a double layer of lipids that is wrapped around the axon many times. This double layer of lipids is also present in cell membranes, as was discovered by structural research using electron microscopes. In addition to facilitating communication between nerve cells, myelin also prevents signals from jumping to unintended nerve cells, which in turn might cause a short circuit.

When you take the brain of professional pianists as an example, they show an increased presence of myelin in the brain areas that are the most relevant for pianists. Furthermore, research shows that the build-up of myelin is a very slow process. This is another indication of how deliberate practice seems to work. It is a process that takes years and then results in unconscious competence (Chap. 10). Small steps that combine to eventually make a big difference.

Research into myelin is still in the early stages, but all indications are that this bodily substance might provide the physical link between intense practice and excellent performance.

5.10 Results of the Study

How important is self-efficacy really? Well, this study shows that self-efficacy is the number one predictor of sustainable performance! Exactly as Bandura had described; self-efficacy as a drive for sustainable performance.

What can we do with this observation? What should we do? And what can we learn from it? The first thing to consider is that self-efficacy is not something that you either have or do not have, it is an attitude. Self-efficacy is an attitude of positive thinking, as Bandura puts it. Or the optimism—performance indicator number 4—about your own ability to complete a specific task. It is this notion that makes the most important result of this study so interesting. Professionals with the right personality not only know how to rely on their skills but can improve those skills through deliberate practice. That enables them to further improve their performance for themselves and for their organizations in the future. Super talents do not exist.

The Dutch CEOs paid very little attention to the number 1 performance predictor. Self-efficacy was only the tenth performance indicator they would use to select professionals!

References

Bandura A (1977) Self-efficacy: toward a unifying theory of behavioral change. Psychol Rev 84(2):191–215

Cohen PR, Feigenbaum EA (2014) The handbook of artificial intelligence. Stanford, CA, HeurisTech Press/Los Altos; CA, William Kaufmann, Inc

Collins J (2001) Good to great. Why some companies make the leap ... and others don't. New York, NY, HarperCollins Publishers

Colvin G (2010) Talent is overrated. Penguin Group, New York, NY

Gladwell M (2005) Blink: the power of thinking without thinking. Little, Brown and Company, New York, NY

Grant A (2016) Originals: how non-conformists move the world. Viking, New York, NY

Kodden S (2014) Be a HERO. How to bring out leadership in everyone. Bernard Daniel Press

Chapter 6
The Relationship Between Work Engagement and Sustainable Performance

Abstract Be engaged, be happy, as the theory of engagement teaches us. To feel that you are doing exactly that where your unique talents and interests lie and where you make optimal use of personal and work-related energy sources. Who does not want to be engaged? And which manager does not desire to have engaged employees? In tough times, engagement provides extra energy to cope with stressful situations, making these employees invaluable to the organization they work in. However, studies into engagement show that almost 90% of the employees interviewed experience this work and life joy to a lesser extent, or not at all.

Keywords Work engagement theory · Personal resources · Work-related resources · Sustainable performance

6.1 Introduction

What makes someone engaged in their work and under which conditions can he or she perform optimally? And is work engagement something that can be taught and/or stimulated? Answers to these questions could help us achieve sustainable performance in our daily lives and provide us with more fun and energy in doing so. Or they could help us to avoid doing things that only lead to stress and negative energy. To what extent are vigor, dedication, and absorption (the three aspects of work engagement) required to recover that energy again, day after day?

And how important is work engagement for sustainable performance? Below is my hypothesis:

Hypothesis 3
Having work engagement to a greater or lesser degree, positively or negatively influences the relationship between talent and performance (Fig 6.1).

© The Author(s) 2020   39
B. Kodden, *The Art of Sustainable Performance*, SpringerBriefs in Business,
https://doi.org/10.1007/978-3-030-46463-9_6

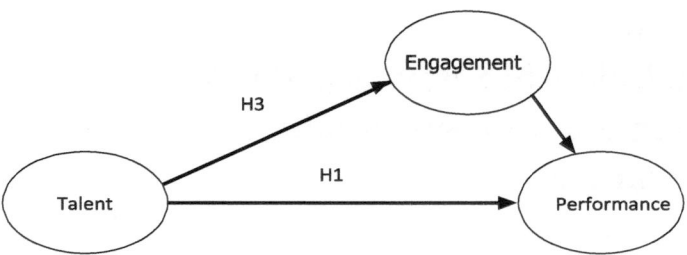

Fig. 6.1 Hypothesis 3

6.2 Success Through Enthusiasm

Studies on work engagement unequivocally show that each success an organization experiences originates from the enthusiasm and passion of its employees. Engaged employees work harder and are more focused (Van Rhenen 2008; Bakker et al. 2009; Kodden and Hupkes 2019; Kodden and Groenveld 2019). This is something organizations will definitely find useful in our current economic climate; achieving more with less people. Engaged employees are also very fit and confident in terms of their private lives (Bakker et al. 2009). They add a lot of value to their employers. But not just for their employers; engaged individuals are more likely to change jobs if they do not feel sufficiently challenged and/or create their own positive feedback by taking on a positive attitude and a great radius of action. Engaged individuals are capable of facing their fears and taking the necessary steps to achieve their final goal.

6.3 The Theory of Work Engagement

Thanks to Einstein, we know that energy forms the basis of everything. Without energy, we would not have raw materials, there could be no labor and there would not be any finished products. Energy is required to manufacture any product that you might find in a store. You also need the energy to achieve great things. The more energy, the better. You have to constantly take action. Never standstill.

The theory of work engagement (Bakker et al. 2009) posits that an engaged employee has a very positive attitude, which is characterized by boundless vitality, energy, and a will to work and invest effort. Engagement is a positive, affective-cognitive state of supreme satisfaction.

Engagement is an attitude towards life that means you try to make the most of your talents and passions using as much vigor, dedication and absorption as possible. *Engage life and live happy*, that is what The theory of work engagement tells us. The feeling that your activities in life perfectly match your unique talents and interests, enabling you to make the most of your energy sources, both at home and at work. Who wouldn't want to feel engaged in daily life? And what employer wouldn't desire engaged employees? In difficult times, work engagement can provide the extra energy required to manage stressful situations, demonstrating how valuable such employees are to their organizations. Yet, studies on work engagement show that less than 20% of surveyed employees fully experience this type of joy in their work and lives. In fact, earlier studies indicated that many professionals have lost their work engagement as a result of their talents not being recognized or the rigid structure of their organization.

6.4 Supreme Satisfaction

According to the theory of work engagement, the state of supreme satisfaction is characterized by vigor, dedication, and absorption. The exact meaning of these three might not be immediately evident, therefore they can be defined as follows:

- "Vigor" refers to high levels of energy, feeling fit and strong, being able to work for long periods without getting tired.
- "Dedication" is all about being strongly involved in one's work. Work is regarded as useful and meaningful, inspiring, and challenging and creates feelings of enthusiasm.
- Lastly, "Absorption" refers to being happily engrossed in one's work, resulting in one losing their sense of time and finding it difficult to detach (Bakker et al. 2009).

Engaged people are open to new ideas, are both physically and mentally healthy, look for their authentic talents, and start every day full of energy and vigor and ready to work. This is not just a positive for the person him or herself, it also stimulates their immediate coworkers and has a positive effect on the organization.

6.5 Highly Energetic Leading Doers

Although the definition of work engagement was and still is very clear (Bakker et al. 2009), my mind went back to the link and my affinity with sports and energy while I was helping young ambitious students transform themselves into future leaders. To me, the new heroes were Highly Energetic Responsible Operators (HERO). One night in 2013, I created my own definition of engaged people, in part because I felt the theory of work engagement was lacking an important aspect of using one's talents. For instance, in the past, I always felt that I was engaged, but I could not always apply my energy in a useful way because I was not using my talents correctly or because I lacked direction. When I took charge of my own life, I rediscovered my talents and my energy. Only then did my performance truly start to improve. That is how I came up with the acronym HERO (Kodden 2014) (Fig. 6.2).

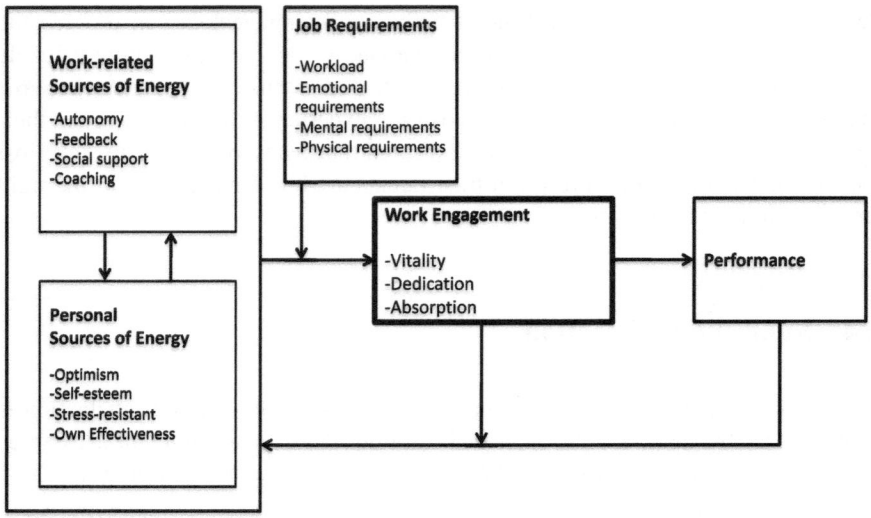

Fig. 6.2 The work engagement model (Bakker et al. 2009)

6.6 Personal Sources of Energy

Longitudinal studies indicate that once people are engaged, they tend to remain that way (Bakker et al. 2009; Kodden and Van Ingen 2019). This is an important conclusion to consider when striving for a positive attitude. People with multiple sources of energy (energy sources that you are personally responsible for, such as optimism, self-esteem, stress resistance, and self-efficacy) are able to better safeguard their own interests and stay intrinsically motivated for a longer time (Xanthoupoulou et al. 2008a, b). They strive to achieve goals because these fit their personal interests and ideas, rather than because other people order them around.

In 2003, Wiese, Rothmann and Storm discovered a positive correlation between personal sources of energy and work engagement in police officers. They appeared to have an active coping style. They were problem-oriented and actively took steps to reduce stress and remain engaged.

Another important discovery was made by Xanthoupoulou (2008a, b). Her team of scientists demonstrated that personal sources of energy have mutually beneficial relation to work-related sources of energy.

The more engaged employees were, the more access they got to additional work-related sources of energy and vice versa. Sources of energy—such as increased autonomy, coaching, and team atmosphere—could be reinforced through optimism and positive energy.

The infectiousness of work engagement is not just limited to work colleagues. For example, it seems very likely that work engagement has a positive influence on the enthusiasm of others. Recent studies show that employees can even influence their partner at home through their enthusiasm (Westman et al. 2011).

As many large-scale studies show, including my own Ph.D. work, work engagements is crucial to (knowledge) organizations. For example, a global survey by Gallup (2013) shows that work engagement has several positive effects on organizations, ensuring:

- Less absenteeism (−37%);
- Fewer accidents (−49%);
- Fewer quality issues (−60%);
- Higher customer satisfaction (+12%);
- Greater productivity (+18%); and
- Higher profits (+16%).

It, therefore, seems that the importance of employees' work engagement for sustainable performance should not be underestimated.

The presence of talent appears to be a prerequisite for performance, but this only explains—in complete accordance with Ericsson and Colvin's theories—a small part of the measured variety of performance levels. The level of engagement, the ability to meet the job requirements, and especially the presence of certain critical personality traits turn out to be much more important(see Appendix B: Important results of the study on performance indicators).

At this stage of my research, my curiosity about the importance of work engagement and its aspects of vigor, dedication, and absorption was as great as ever. To what degree do these elements, in addition to talent and other performance indicators, influence sustainable performance today (Fig. 6.3)?

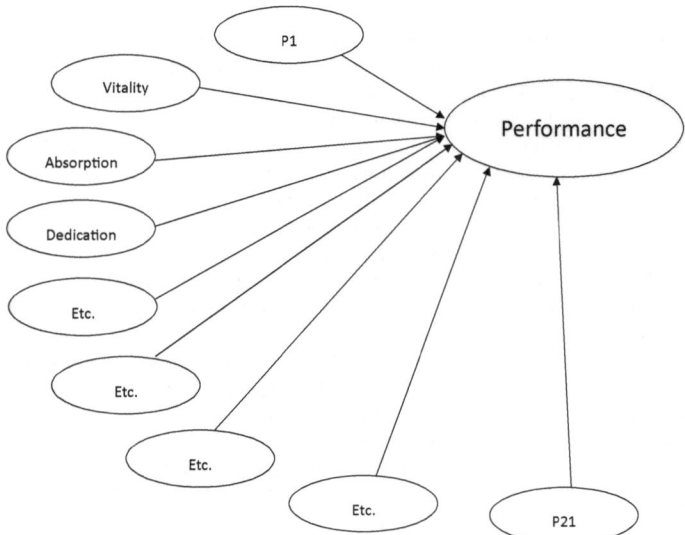

Fig. 6.3 Study on performance indicators and the three aspects of work engagement

6.7   Results of the Study

This study unequivocally shows that employees' work engagement is vital to performance. Of the five variables (talent, personality traits, fit with the organization, work engagement, and job requirements), the level of engagement—following certain specific personality traits—is the most important indicator for organizations in order to achieve new results. Moreover, these specific personality traits turn out to influence the level of engagement. One and one makes three, it seems!

Engaged employees perform better, that much is clear. As this study has shown, dedication (the number 6 performance predictor) and vigor (number 7) are especially crucial for sustainable performance!

Which specific personal trait is then the most important predictor for work engagement? Intrinsic motivation! My study shows that intrinsically motivated people also have higher levels of work engagement. This is in accordance with Daniel Pink's theory (2009).

The Dutch CEOs did pay particular attention to this performance indicator and rated the elements of dedication and absorption of work engagement as number 6 and number 13, respectively, of the most important selection criteria. They do not consider the vigor of candidates as important as has been suggested by this study. Dutch CEOs place vigor at the 11th place of important selection criteria!

References

Bakker A, Schaufeli W, Van Rhenen W (2009) How changes in job demands and resources predict burnout, work engagement, and sickness absenteeism. J Organ Behav

Gallup (2013) Worldwide, 13% of employees are engaged at work. http://www.gallup.com/poll/165269/worldwide-employees-engaged-work.aspx

Kodden S (2014) Be a HERO. How to bring out leadership in everyone. Bernard Daniel Press

Kodden B, Groenweg B (2019) The mediating effect of work engagement on the relationship between person-organization fit and knowledge sharing. J Appl Bus Econ 21(8)

Kodden B, Hupkes L (2019) Organizational environment, personal resources and work engagement as predictors of coaching performance. J Manag Policy Pract 20(3)

Pink D (2009) The surprising truth about what motivates us. Riverhead Books

van Rhenen W (2008) From stress to engagement (Thesis University of Amsterdam). Consulted at http://dare.uva.nl/document/107037

Westman M, Bakker A, Roziner I, Sonnentag S (2011) Crossover of job demands and emotional exhaustion within teams: a longitudinal multilevel study. Anxiety, Stress Coping 24(5):561–577

Wiese L, Rothmann S, Storm K (2003) Coping, stress and burnout in the South African police service in Kwazulu-natal. SA J Industr Psychol

Xanthopoulou D, Bakker AB, Heuven E, Demerouti E, Schaufeli WB (2008a) Working in the sky: a diary study among flight attendants. J Occup Health Psychol 13(4):345–356

Xanthopoulou D, Bakker AB, Demerouti E, Schaufeli WB (2008b) How job and personal resources influence work engagement and financial returns: a diary study in a Greek fast-food company. J Occup Organ Psychol 82(1):183–200

Chapter 7
Nurturing Employee Vigor: Implications for Sustainable Performance

Abstract The theory of engagement posits that an engaged employee has a highly positive attitude that is characterized by an unparalleled zest for life, energy, the will to work, and to commit themselves fully. This allows the employee to achieve special performances. Those who are engaged, are open to new ideas, are both physically and mentally healthy, look for their authentic talents, and start every new (work)day with plenty of energy and a zest for life. This is not only pleasant for the individual themselves, but also inspiring for their immediate colleagues and beneficial to the organization.

Keywords Vigor · Work engagement · Theory · Performance indicators · Sustainable performance

7.1 Introduction

The labor market is rapidly changing and in the next thirty years, the potential professional population will decrease by three-quarters of a million, according to Dutch agency CBS (2015). While the number of elderly people increases, the number of working people decreases. This requires sustainable and wide employment of the total present amount of available energy, also at a macro-economic level. Consequently, employers and employees must take their responsibility and make sure that they utilize this energy optimally. I believe in the power of energy management as contributing towards sustainable employability and wide talent development. Vitality of body and mind, and care and attention to these factors are essential components of self-development and development of your talents. A strategic view on energy management, that is carried on both the highest and the lowest level in the organization, is a prerequisite. Sustainable talent development plays an essential role here. Employees are motivated, stimulated, and facilitated to work on their own fitness and vitality (Kodden 2014).

Involvement from all departments, the board, and possibly also the board of directors and support from a work's council are a determining factor for success (Kodden and Hupkes 2019; Kodden and Groenveld 2019). Everyone must contribute to energy management. A fitness program, set up specially and attuned individually, must not be seen as an expenditure, but as an investment that will redeem itself in various fields. A program at Ernst and Young (2017) resulted in employees becoming 85% fitter, 75% had improved their stamina, and 63% of participants experienced a better energy balance. 51% indicated that they were able to work in a more focused way as a result.

Vital people perform better and enjoy things more. According to research conducted by Diehl and Stoffelsen (2007), vital employees do not only look happier, they also seem to do things with little or no effort, have practically no complaints, recover faster, and have plenty of energy left at the end of the day. Vitality and energy management sound much more positive to most people than the words health and working conditions. Who does not want to have more energy left at the end of the day? For instance to exercise.

The word "vigor" is becoming increasingly common. The term can be applied to much more than just sports and health. So what exactly is vigor? Does it have to do with:

- Being productive;
- Being sustainably employable;
- Being fit;
- Being young at heart;
- Being healthy;
- Showing resilience;
- Being happy;
- Being engaged or;
- Being willing to change?

Many of these concepts come close to the meaning of "vigor," yet do not quite cover it. Instead, they are phenomena that are often a cause or result of that vigor. It could be claimed that, in addition to talent, you also need a good physical and mental fit in order to achieve sustainable performance. That is why my fourth hypothesis goes as follows:

Hypothesis 4
Having a good fit to the physical and mental job requirements to a greater or lesser degree positively or negatively influences the relationship between talent and performance (Fig. 7.1).

7.2   Energy and Motivation

Vigor is often about vitality. Many descriptions of vitality point to the Latin word *vita*, meaning "life," as in life force, liveliness, lust for life, life energy, etc. Ryan and Frederick (1997) confirm this and describe subjective vitality as the conscious experience of one's being alive: *aliveness* and positive energy. According to Bakker et al. (2009), vigor stands for energetic, resilient, fit, and working without getting

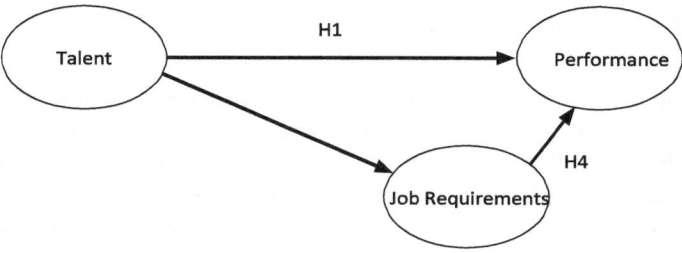

Fig. 7.1 Hypothesis 4

tired. Vigorous and dedicated people can make the difference, I concluded in *Become a HERO* (2014). Quality over quantity. Furthermore, a variety of studies show that the level of work engagement and being able to meet demanding job requirements are strongly linked.

Vigor is, therefore, more than the absence of illness. Vigor is more than being physically fit and therefore not the same as being healthy and/or the absence of an unhealthy lifestyle that might include smoking, not exercising, eating too much, or drinking too much. Vigor is a combination of energy and motivation and appears to ensure sustainable employability of employees. It also influences the extent to which they are able to meet the physical and mental requirements of a job, as well as how willing and able they are to keep doing their current and future jobs (Kodden and Hupkes 2019).

7.3   The Hedgehog Concept

In my earlier book, I explained having talents and being able to meet mental and physical job requirements. The main idea of my book *Become a HERO* (2014) is similar to Jim Collins' hedgehog concept (2001); the metaphor for the idea that once you discover what you can become best at, when you truly understand what you can make money doing, and really know what makes you passionate, you can overcome any obstacle. Collins uses the story of the hedgehog that was attacked by a smart, sly, and agile fox on a daily basis. By using its only weapon, its spines, the fox did not have a chance to harm the hedgehog. Despite the fact that the hedgehog was slow, small, and not very smart, the fox had no way to counter its spines.

Once you know what your strengths are and how you can develop them further, you will notice that you will become even more engaged. According to Collins, your lust for life, and even your life expectancy will increase. You will be happier going to work, will have more energy to give it your all and you will be better able to meet all your job requirements.

7.4   The Need for Vigor

It seems vigor is necessary in order to become engaged. A high level of energy is required to enable you to become active—and stay active—to achieve your goals (Ryan and Frederick 1997). This is why vigor is an important aspect of work engagement, in addition to dedication and absorption. A study by the University of South Carolina shows that running, rowing, and other sports that make you sweat are not just good for your body, but also for your brain. Running for half an hour three or four times a week is already enough to keep your brain in shape and even delay early Alzheimer's (Charvat 2009). Higher grades, fewer mistakes, improving your math, forgetting less; intense exercise keeps your body fit and your brain young (Van Vuuren 2011).

Exercise not only stimulates your mind but your brain as well. "Especially children, who are in an important stage of development, become smarter when they exercise and play outside. In particular, when their activities require concentration, communication and coordination," according to Jaap Seidell, professor at the Vrije Universiteitin Amsterdam (Seidell 2012).

"Basically, it is about the step from not exercising at all, to half an hour of moderate exercise every day. That provides the greatest benefit.'"

Seidell (2012) acknowledges that few people feel like leaving the house to exercise after a hard day's work. "But if those people take their dog for a walk, they return happier than when they left. It is important to teach this behavior at an early age. If you have not done this all your life and you are overweight, suffer from bad knees or shortness of breath, starting to exercise can be very difficult. That is why it is so important to stay active, from early childhood to old age."

7.5   Focus

Many people would agree that to become and stay vigorous, you indeed need to exercise regularly. But according to Tony Schwartz, founder and CEO of The Energy Project and regular contributor to the *Harvard Business Review*, the key is to not just exercise. In order to stay vigorous, you also need to add focus to your life. Not easy, considering the fact that our modern lives require us to multitask. Work, parenting, maintaining a social life; but do not forget to exercise. All preferably on the same day. Staying vigorous is all about applying focus. In his studies, Schwartz demonstrates that the productivity of individual employees decreases by about 25% when they perform multiple tasks at the same time. Several other studies have also shown that multitasking does not work and can even be counterproductive (Schwarz 2012).

The number of Dutch people who are overworked or suffering from burnout is increasing rapidly. Most people don't exactly remember the process that led to their current situation, but a lot of people who've suffered from burnout in the past remember exactly when things went wrong. Much has been published in recent years on the symptoms of burnout; psychiatrists, doctors, therapists, researchers, consultants, and former patients have all provided insights on the issue.

According to the Dutch statistics bureau, 14% of employees in the Netherlands reported burnout symptoms in 2014. That is one in seven. At least several times a month, they felt empty after work, emotionally drained by their job or tired when they were confronted with work while waking up. Note that burnout symptoms are approximately equally common in all employees of all age groups between 25 and 65 years of age CBS 2015). Other research by the Dutch statistics bureau shows that burnouts are more prevalent among higher-educated than less-educated employees. It also shows how burnouts are related to certain personality traits and the lack of certain work-related sources of energy. As my colleague, Professor Van Rhenen explains: "You can prevent a burnout through life and work engagement." Only do things that suit you as a person and continue to exercise. Together, this will give you more energy and will make you stronger instead of weaker (van Rhenen 2008).

Luckily, science in the Netherlands is also increasingly recognizing the importance of vitality. In 2010, Tinka van Vuuren was even appointed as professor of vitality management at the Open University in Heerlen. Her speech was aptly titled *You don't have to be sick to get better* (2012). In it, she emphasized the importance of vitality management. "Employers who ignore the vitality of their employees will get in real trouble in the coming years," she said.

7.6 Vigor and Self-efficacy

You also need self-efficacy to start exercising. In this case, it means that you consider yourself able to execute the desired behavior (exercising). Self-efficacy, therefore, comes from the combination of self-confidence—I will be able to sport for an hour in the gym—and actually carrying out the intended activity (making time to exercise). As I have described before, self-efficacy—having the necessary skills to perform a certain task and the confidence in one's ability to successfully complete it—differs from self-confidence in that self-confidence refers to believing in oneself, whereas self-efficacy concerns one's perceived ability to complete a certain task. Believing in one's own ability leads to positive intentions actually resulting in new behavior and sustainable performance.

Fourteen Reasons to Exercise

Exercise makes it easier for your body to draw oxygen from the air and transport it to your muscles. Every year, you lose about 1% of this capacity. This means a lot of heavy breathing once you pass thirty. Exercise can cut this loss in half.

1. Exercises lower blood pressure by keeping the vascular system healthy.
2. Regular exercise improves your body's ability to metabolize glucose. This decreases the risk of type 2 diabetes.
3. Exercise maintains your immune system and counteracts aging.

4. Exercise breaks down body fat. In addition, the muscles you build up through exercise increase your metabolic rate.

5. Exercise maintains bone strength. Bone density decreases by 1% every year. An hour of weight lifting a week is enough to strengthen your bones.

6. Exercise strengthens muscle.

7. Stretch exercises like those in yoga or tai chi prevent arthritis.

8. When we exercise, we sleep better. Active during the day, tired at night.

9. It makes us happy. Exercise releases endorphins and reduces the risk of depression.

10. Endorphins also reduce anxiety.

11. Regular exercise will keep you healthier and reduce the amount of sick days you need.

12. Exercise improves memory.

13. Exercise reduces the risk of dementia.

14. But above all, exercise gives you more energy. You will feel less tired and less stressed.

7.7   Results of the Study

As I described in Chap. 5, self-efficacy turns out to be the number one predictor for sustainable performance. Vigor also seems to be very important for sustainable performance by professionals and is number 7 on the list of performance predictors. My research also shows that both are strongly interconnected. Other studies also show that the combination of both is the key to sustainable performance. Self-efficacy and vigor start with focusing on yourself, on your personal development.

This study not only shows that vigor is important for sustainable performance as an element of work engagement, but also that it is important for the fit with the mental job requirements. After self-efficacy and adaptability, it is the third most important predictor of sustainable performance. The importance of vigor and the ability to handle the physical and especially mental job requirements can therefore not be stressed enough.

The Dutch CEOs, however, paid little attention to this important predictor of performance. The fit with the mental job requirements did not even make their top 15.

It seems therefore that it is high time for Dutch organizations to develop a new approach to talent and performance management. A perspective that attaches more value to the importance of vigor and employees' abilities to meet the physical and especially mental requirements of the job. Not only are our jobs and organizations changing increasingly fast, job requirements are also becoming more demanding. Organizations that ensure the physical and mental resilience of their workforce seem better equipped to meet today's requirements for sustainable performance.

References

Bakker A, Schaufeli W, Van Rhenen W (2009) How changes in job demands and resources predict burnout, work engagement, and sickness absenteeism. J Organ Behav

CBS (2015) Eén op de zeven werknemers heeft burn-outklachten. https://www.cbs.nl/nl-nl/nieuws/2015/47/cbs-en-tno-een-op-de-zeven-werknemers-heeft-burn-outklachten

Charvat M (2009) Why exercise is good for your brain. psychology today

Collins J (2001) Good to great. Why some companies make the leap ... and others don't. HarperCollins Publishers, New York, NY

Diehl PJ, Stoffelsen JM (2007) Vitaliteit en arbeid in 100 vragen. Kluwer, Alphen aanden Rijn

Ernst & Young (2017). A global study on work-life challenges across generations

Huang T, Larsen KT, Möller NC, Andersen LB (2013) The effects of physical activity and exercise on brain-derived neurotrophic factor in healthy humans: a review

Kodden S (2014) Be a HERO. How to bring out leadership in everyone. Bernard Daniel Press

Kodden B, Groenweg B (2019) The mediating effect of work engagement on the relationship between person-organization fit and knowledge sharing. J Appl Bus Econ 21(8)

Kodden B, Hupkes L (2019) Organizational environment, personal resources and work engagement as predictors of coaching performance. J Manag Policy Pract 20(3). https://doi.org/10.33423/jmpp.v20i3.2230

Ryan RM, Frederick C (1997) On energy, personality, and health: subjective vitality as a dynamic reflection of w-being. J Pers 65(3):529–565

Schaufeli WB, Bakker AB (2007) Burnout en bevlogenheid. In: Schau-feli WB, Bakker AB (eds) Depsychologievanarbeidengezondheid, pp 341–358. Houten: Bohn Stafleu vanLoghum

Schwarz T (2012) The magic of doing one thing at a time. Consulted at http://blogs.hbr.org/2012/03/the-magic-of-doing-one-thing-a/

Seidell J (2012) Sporten maakt je slim? In broadcast https://www.bnr.nl/radio/10178252/sporten-maakt-je-slim?disableUserNav=true

van Rhenen W (2008) From stress to engagement (Thesis University of Amsterdam). Consulted at http://dare.uva.nl/document/107037

van Vuuren T (2011) Je hoeft niet ziek te zijn om beter te worden (oration). Open University Heerlen, Heerlen

Chapter 8
The Effect of Person-Organization Fit on Work Engagement and Performance

Abstract Perceived organizational fit as perceived by employees can function as an important distal organizational resource, which has motivational potential and can foster employee's work engagement. Based on the theoretical lens, this study examines mechanisms that can explain the motivational potential that the organizational environment and personal resources might have at both the individual as the team level.

Keywords Organizational fit · P-O fit theory · Performance indicators · Sustainable performance

8.1 Introduction

It seems that the importance of physical and mental vigor for professional and organizational development is clear. But we should not underestimate the importance of a good fit with the corporate culture, as many other studies show (Kristof 1996; Kristof-Brown et al. 2002; Taris 2003). My fifth hypothesis was as follows:

Hypothesis 5 Having a good fit with the organization to a greater or a lesser degree positively or negatively influences the relationship between talent and performance.

Many scientists and authors support this hypothesis. Take Kristof-Brown and Taris, for instance, who have put the importance of person-organization fit (P-O fit) on the scientific map (Fig. 8.1).

Their P-O fit studies are based on the idea that individuals are increasingly interacting with their environment, and that employee behavior is influenced and directed by both environment factors and personality traits. The current interest in P-O fit studies can also be explained through the fact that several researchers, including the aforementioned Kristof (1996) and Taris (2003) are finding conformation for the assumption that a high degree of fit of the employee with his environment, has a positive effect on both his own performance and that of the organization. But what aspects determine whether an employee has a good fit with an organization? And to what extent are these elements on their own important for sustainable performance?

© The Author(s) 2020

B. Kodden, *The Art of Sustainable Performance*, SpringerBriefs in Business,
https://doi.org/10.1007/978-3-030-46463-9_8

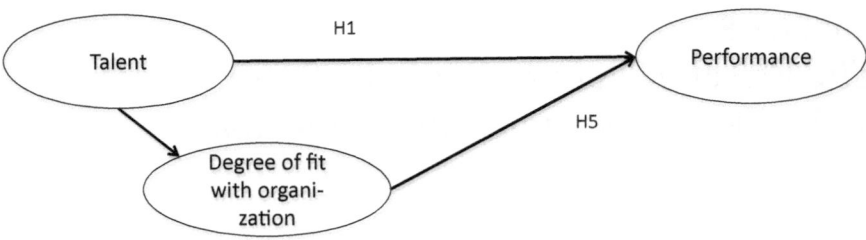

Fig. 8.1 Hypothesis 5

8.2 Fit with Job and Supervisor

The Interaction Processing meta-theory by Ehrhart and Ziegert (2005) describes how and why the attractiveness of organizations is influenced. This theory is basically a framework for all theories that argue that the fit between personal and environmental characteristics makes organizations more attractive for employees. In the literature, this fit is called the Person-Environment Fit (P-E fit).In a broader sense, P-E fit can be defined as the match between the values, goals, and personality of an individual and those of that person's environment (Kristof-Brown et al. 2002).

The term "environment" in the definition of P-E fit above, is a very wide-ranging concept. It is therefore important to split up "environment" into different domains (Kristof-Brown et al. 2002). The Person-Job Fit is about the match between a person and his or her job, just like P-O fit is about a person and the culture of the organization he or she works for. Finally, there is also a Person-Supervisor Fit. In my study, I used the following important selection criteria: a good fit with the job and the culture of the organization and supervisor. At the end of this chapter, I will discuss the results individually.

8.3 Organizational Culture and Change

How important is organizational culture? And to what extent does a good fit with the organizational culture determine sustainable performance? The most famous management authors on these topics are probably Cameron and Quinn (2011). Kim Cameron is a professor of management and organization at the University of Michigan. His studies on organizational performance, corporate culture, and the development of leadership have resulted in over 120 articles and 14 books. His most recent study is aimed at the positive dynamic that leads to improved performance in organizations. As an instructor and researcher, he is mostly interested in organizational change and effectiveness. Robert Quinn is associated with the Graduate School of Business of the University of Michigan. He is internationally recognized as the leading authority in the field of change management. Quinn's research and education are aimed at change and effectiveness in organizations. He is mostly known for his

Competing Values Framework (the Quinn model), which is considered to be one of the most important models in the history of the business.

According to Cameron and Quinn, no twenty-first century organization should be proud of being consistent, remaining unchanged, and still being in the same position it was a decade earlier. They believe stability is more a form of stagnation than a goal of equanimity or as Billy Beane put it: "No matter how successful you are, change is always good."

Yet most planned organizational changes fail at an alarming rate. According to several studies on organizational change, up to three-quarters of all attempts fail completely, in many cases threatening the survival of the organization. However, what is interesting about these failures, according to Cameron and Quinn, are the causes that have been cited for the lack of success. Several studies show that disregarding organizational culture was most often identified as the cause of failure (Cameron and Quinn 2011).

8.4 Conditions for Success

A significant amount of the somewhat dated literature indicates that successful businesses—those that continually make a profit and achieve above-average turnover—need to meet at least several of the following clearly described conditions (Cameron and Quinn 2011):

1. High barriers to entry for new entrants;
2. Unique products;
3. Having a large market share;
4. Limited bargaining power of customers;
5. Limited bargaining power of suppliers;
6. Significant rivalry between competitors (instead of towards your organization).

This makes it all the more remarkable that the most successful American businesses—and I expect the situation in Europe and the Netherlands will not be all that different—of the past thirty years had none of these competitive advantages (Cameron and Quinn 2011). Of the best-performing businesses of the past three decades—the ones that completely outperformed the competition—none met even one of the previously mentioned conditions for success.

Apple, which nearly went bankrupt in 1998, is one of the five most valuable companies in the world, worth more than Microsoft. Apple entered a market that was dominated by established and highly competitive companies such as Microsoft, Motorola, Nokia, IBM, and Dell. The same was true for animation studio Pixar, which entered a market that had long been dominated by Disney. In less than 30 years of its existence, the company scored 11 hit movies out of 11 attempts. This was completely unheard of in the movie industry. Every movie Pixar has made has been nominated for an Oscar. It won the award in three out of every four cases. Cameron and Quinn (2011), but also scientists like Taris (2003) and Kristof-Brown (2005), indicate that it is the fit with an organization, its culture, and style that determines sustainable performance. Organizations with a strong culture and employees that suit it have the greatest chance to survive according to the aforementioned scientists.

But how important is a good fit with the organization and the organizational culture really? To what extent is a good fit with their immediate supervisors important for the performance of professionals?

In this study, organizational culture was defined as the collection of norms, values, and behavior that is shared by the organization's members, and that connects the members to each other and the organization.

8.5 Results of the Study

Realizing and maintaining a culture of performance with the right principles, norms, and values are vital to sustainable performance. Studies confirm this again and again. According to scientists Cameron and Quinn, these aspects are in fact the most important factor for the success or failure of any organization (Cameron and Quinn 1998, 2011). Without a fitting culture, that is embraced and reinforced by every new hire, the work effectiveness of the organization will quickly diminish, eventually leading to the organization's downfall.

The outcomes of this study also confirm this statement. The overall concept of Organization Fit (fit with the culture and supervisor) showed a very strong and significant correlation to performance (also see Appendices C and D: Correlation Matrix Factors). The results of this study did not specifically indicate that a fit with the organizational culture is the most important performance criterion. A good fit with the supervisor scored much higher as a performance predictor.

It turns out that sustainable performance is significantly influenced not just by organizational culture, but also by the way a team is managed by its supervisor. People make decisions for, perform for, and leave because of other people, it seems. Getting along with one's supervisor appears to be essential for sustainable performance.

References

Cameron KS, Quinn RE (1988) Paradox and transformation: toward a theory of change in organization and management. Eds. Cambridge, MA, Ballinger

Cameron KS, Quinn RE (2011) Onderzoeken en veranderen van organisatiecultuur (3rd revised edition). Academic Service, The Hague

Ehrhart KH, Ziegert JC (2005) Why are individuals attracted to organizations? J Manag 31(6):901–919

Kristof AL (1996) Person-organization fit: an integrative review of its conceptualizations, measurement and implications. Personn Psychol 49(1):1–49

Kristof-Brown AL, Jansen KJ, Colbert AE (2002) A policy-capturing study of the simultaneous effects of fit with jobs, groups and organizations. J Appl Psychol 87(5):985–993

Taris R (2003) Person-environment fit. A longitudinal study of the interaction between employee characteristics and work environmental characteristics. Ridderprint Offsetdrukkerij, Ridderkerk

Chapter 9
Performance Culture: The Organization as a Tribe

Abstract The continuing success of exceptionally successful businesses has, according to scholar as Cameron and Quinn (1998, 2011), less to do with the influences of the market it is operating in, than with the company's own values. It is not so much about the competition than about personal beliefs, less about means than about vision. Despite the obvious importance of strategy, market presentation or technological innovations, exceptionally successful companies capitalize on something else; the powerful influence of a well-developed and managed unique corporate culture.

Keywords Organizational culture · Performance indicators · Sustainable performance

9.1 Tribal Cultures

Just like in the past, anthropologists Danielle Braun and Jitske Kramer could have easily said. Their bestseller *The Corporate Tribe* (2016), was even named Management Book of the Year in 2016. It is a beautifully written book about the importance of (organizational) culture and the personal fit of individual group members with their tribal culture. In anthropology, a *tribe* refers to a group of related families or clans, subgroups. The most important connecting element of a tribe is its culture, its shared language and religion (Braun and Kramer 2016).

But exactly how can a strong culture of performance be achieved? According to Braun and Kramer, to understand how organizations operate, we need to return to the basic building blocks of these constructs—human beings. We need to look at more than just the psychology of the individual. The focus should be on human beings as pack animals. Organizations consist of groups of people. Anthropologically speaking, an organization consists of different tribes, each with their own chief, rituals, and rules. If we want to understand, influence, change, and/or manage groups, we must understand how people operate. As Marcel Proust puts it, "The real voyage of discovery, consists not of seeking new landscapes, but of having new eyes (Braun and Kramer 2016)."

My quest for sustainable performance continued. I came across the most successful tribe, many say even the most successful organization in recent decades: The All

© The Author(s) 2020

B. Kodden, *The Art of Sustainable Performance*, SpringerBriefs in Business,

https://doi.org/10.1007/978-3-030-46463-9_9

Blacks. Their customs, rituals, and manners, combined with the results of my three-year quantitative study of performance characteristics and selection criteria among Dutch professionals, led to new and surprising insights concerning the benefit of a strong performance culture in our own organizations.

In his book *Legacy* (2013), James Kerr beautifully describes how the New Zealand national rugby team is able to continue on winning. The All Blacks are the most successful rugby team in history but are also considered the most successful sports team in general. Their win rate of 86% is unequaled. Even now, the All Blacks are the reigning world champions. How are they able to do it, again and again? New Zealand cannot be the largest rugby nation with the most available talent to draw from, right? What is the secret to their success? How does the team go from victory to victory? And what can they teach us?

James Kerr believes that the All Blacks are so successful because they select the right people, define the right goal, and maintain the right culture. For several years, Kerr was allowed into the All Blacks' inner circle in order to record their legacy. In his book, Kerr describes 15 leadership lessons that we can all use to achieve higher performance.

Naturally, my main question was *how* the All Blacks select their players. Could they perhaps use similar ideas and performance criteria that I found to be important? The answer was a vowedly yes (although the All Blacks use very different terminology, of course)! "Talent was irrelevant. We carefully picked the players. We used *matrices* to back intuition because there are certain *stats* in rugby that determine a players "*character*," says former coach Wayne Smith.

From victory to victory; it requires a goal and a fit to the job requirements (1), ownership and development of your most important personality traits (2), a sense of connection to each other and to the organization (3), and last but not least, engagement; a positive attitude to life and an attitude of great personal prestige (4). The All Blacks even have a perfect word for it: *mana*. "Talent is good, character is better." More about that later. After all, for the All Blacks, it all starts with that initial concept, the higher purpose, and the fit with the job requirements: *whakapapa*!

9.2 Whakapapa: The Higher Purpose

The All Blacks' success story starts in the small rural town of Christchurch in 1997. Christchurch is where the heart of the now extremely successful team is located. Several players and coaches of the local Crusaders were born there. Wayne Smith says: "Back in 1997, professional rugby was still a long way off. That was certainly true for Christchurch. The Crusaders had had a very poor start to their season, and there was no existing culture to build on." No reason, no purpose, and no well-established principles. The players were simply going through the motions. The Crusaders were having an identity crisis (Kerr 2013).

Wayne Smith: "The more you have to play for, the better you play. It is about purpose and personal meaning…Those are the two big things." The emotional glue in any culture—of a religion, country, or sports team—is its identity and purpose. "The things we consider important to ourselves—our deepest values—have the emotional power to shape behavior." Smith coached the Crusaders to two titles in 1998 and 1999 before he was appointed coach of the All Blacks (Kerr 2013).

This connection between personal values and a higher purpose is something that drives the All Blacks to an almost obsessive degree. When the team members' values are linked to the values and goals of the organization, they will put in more effort to achieve those.

When they do not, it will negatively affect their personal motivation, and eventually the survival of the organization as well. Organizing always starts *inside out*; by formulating a higher purpose."Being part of the legacy," as the All Blacks put it (Kerr 2013).

Several other authors and scientists support this concept, including Pink (2011), Sinek (2009), and Maslow (1943). In the end, it is all about purpose; the why, the meaning of it all. This was also demonstrated by the research and work of Frankl (1946):

> "When asked what they found to be the most important part of their job, 16% of respondents answered, 'earning a lot of money'; 78% indicated that their main and higher purpose was, 'finding meaning and purpose in my life.'"

How do you think the current generation of young professionals would respond to this survey? Finding a sense of purpose and meaning for ourselves and our organizations has only gotten more important! Just like with the All Blacks.

9.3 Ubuntu: Connection to Others and the Organization

According to retired bishop Desmond Tutu, "Ubuntu is the essence of our human existence". It is about our connection to others. The impossibility of living in isolation as human beings. Ubuntu is an ethical or humanist philosophy from sub-Saharan Africa about dedication and relationships between people. The word occurs in the Bantu languages of southern Africa and is considered a traditional African concept. Still, the New Zealand Maoris embraced this important concept as the core of their own culture (Kerr 2013).

Ubuntu is not about having your own goals or your own interests, as Nelson Mandela also explained in an interview with journalist Tim Modesi (Kerr 2013)."But you do it in a way that enables the community around you to improve itself. Those are the most important things in life." Ubuntu means that we send ripples through the greater community, knowing that our actions affect everyone, not just ourselves.

But then what was that "why," that higher purpose (the whakapapa) and the connectedness (Ubuntu) of the All Blacks? How did they define it in order to win everything that could be won? Officially, according to NZRU sources, their initial purpose was "to unite and inspire New Zealand." However, every All Black knows that it goes far beyond that. Their ultimate higher purpose is very simple: "To add to the legacy. To leave the jersey in a better place."

"There now is a rich tradition of players who contributed and continue to contribute to this higher purpose, our legacy," says Wayne Smith. "They stood for and stand for the idea that it is about leaving your uniform, your black jersey in a better state than your predecessor left it in."

"The only thing I did," tells legendary former All Blacks captain Sean Fitzpatrick, "was to leave an even better team to my successors, the next generation of All Blacks. All that was required was a single word; winning."

9.4 Whanau: Ownership

From winning to winning. "Pass the ball," as James Kerr writes in *Legacy* (2013). A shared responsibility (*partnership*) means shared ownership. But it also means personal ownership and development of your most important personality traits. A kind of connection in which each individual is much more willing to give up parts of themselves, all for the greater good. The All Blacks are all owners of what happens on the field and know how to optimally use their most important personality traits to achieve success.

Haka

Haka is the name of a group of ceremonial Maori dances from New Zealand (hakas are also danced on Samoa and Fiji). During a haka, a certain text is spoken. With the dance and the words, they appeal to the gods (forefathers). It is often wrongly thought that the haka is always a war dance. A war dance (the Peruperu) does exist, but there are also hakas for, for instance, funerals. Hakas are performed during all kinds of occasions. For example, tourists can be welcomed to the traditional hangi, a welcoming dinner, with a haka. Hakas are also performed during certain festivities or sports matches. Certain dances are set, others allow dancers the freedom to express themselves however they want.

The dance itself consists of a range of gestures, often starting with knees bent and feet apart. The dancer then flexes his or her muscles and beats them (for instance starting with chest, moving to the arms and thighs). They also use a yanking motion aimed at the heavens to pull down the power of the gods into the warrior. In addition they use varying facial expressions, like rolling back their eyes and showing their tongues.

The Ka Mate is probably the most famous Haka. For years, it has been used by the All Blacks before the start of every match. Nowadays, they sometimes also perform the controversial Kapa o Pango or other hakas. Several other teams from the region also perform this ritual.

9.5   Mana: Talent Is Good, Character Is Better

"Talent is irrelevant. It is all about purpose and personal meaning... Leaders don't create followers," According to management scientist and leadership guru Peters (2005). "They create more leaders." Group members who feel ownership of a shared purpose and realize that everyone might (have to) play the most important role in the team. In 2011, this happened to Stephen Donald, considered by many to be one of the greatest rugby talents in the world. A year earlier, Donald thought that he had played his last match for the All Blacks. During an earlier, crucial match against Australia, his performance was—to put it mildly—unsatisfactory. His coach had not used him since then. So, during the 2011 world championships, he spent his time fishing in the Waikato-river.

However, a string of bad luck for the All Blacks during this championship would change Stephen Donald's life in a spectacular fashion. First, Dan Carter—one of the most talented and the highest scoring rugby player in the history of the sport—became injured. This was a major loss to the team. Soon after, the same thing happened to Colin Shade. New Zealand was in a panic. With only one experienced fly half (an important position in rugby and the person who also takes free kicks) left. The All Blacks were in serious trouble. All Blacks coach Graham Henry picked up the phone right away and called Stephen Donald: "Get over here!" (Kerr 2013).

In the 43rd min, during the final against France, the last remaining experienced fly half and free kick taker, Aaron Cruden, had to leave the pitch. Murphy's law seemed very real for New Zealand at that moment. A day after he had been fishing, having barely trained for weeks, Stephen Donald was called up as a substitute. He was wearing a borrowed All Blacks jersey two sizes too small. The whole country held its breath.

In one of the most exciting finals ever, the French allowed a penalty in the final minutes of the game. The most important moment for any free kick specialist had arrived. Without even being asked, Stephen Donald stepped up to the ball, eyed both goal posts, and ... scored! New Zealand's fourth choice, who had not played for even a minute in six weeks, became the pride of the nation that day. He has been a hero to the All Blacks and its supporters ever since (Kerr 2013).

Whakapapa, Ubuntu, Whanau, and Mana. Leaders create leaders. People who feel a connection to a higher purpose, who feel ownership of the tasks that they, regardless of circumstances, have to perform. People who show the right attitude for sustainable performance: "Talent is good, character is better!"

References

Braun D, Kramer J (2016) The corporate tribe: organizational lessons froms anthropology. Routledge

Cameron KS, Quinn RE (1988) Paradox and transformation: toward a theory of change in organization and management. Ballinger, Cambridge, MA

Cameron KS, Quinn RE (2011) Onderzoeken en veranderen van organisatiecultuur, vol 3. Academic Service, The Hague

Frankl V (1946) Man's search for meaning. The classic tribute to hope from the Holocaust

Kerr J (2013) Legacy. What the all blacks can teach us about the business of life. Constable and Robinson Ltd., London

Maslow AH (1943) A theory of human motivation. Psychol Rev 50(4):370–396

Peters T (2005) Leadership. DK Publishers

Pink D (2011) Drive. The surprising truth about what motivates us. Riverhead Books

Sinek S (2009) Start with why. Penguin Books Ltd., New York

Chapter 10
The Art of Sustainable Performance: The Zeigarnik Effect

Abstract Why does one organization remain successful while others are falling apart or just disappear? Why is one person successful over and over again, while no one expected him or her to be? The secret of winning persons and teams seems to lie in performance indicators and personality traits, on which—strangely enough—many organizations just do not select their employees.

Keywords Personality traits · Performance indicators · Recruitment · Selection · Sustainable performance

10.1 The Brilliant Waiter

Huh, the Zeigarnik effect? You might be wondering what that is. And what does it have to do with the study on performance indicators and personality traits so far? In order to answer these questions, we have to take a trip back in time. It is the mid-twentieth century. Near Berlin University, a large group of university staff decides to have dinner in a local restaurant. Among them are the legendary professor Kurt Lewin, founder of Positive Psychology, and a doctoral student of his called Bluma Zeigarnik. A holiday that would go down in history as the moment when a new scientific phenomenon "emerged" that would later be known as the Zeigarnik effect. The story led to a theory that explained why some soccer players become legends, why some musicians become stars, and some scientists become geniuses. Their secret? The Zeigarnik effect!

Bluma Zeigarnik, her professor and her doctoral thesis supervisor Kurt Lewin, and the other scientists were celebrating in a Berlin restaurant. They ate, drank, and ordered all their drinks, starters, mains, and desserts from the same waiter. Yet he never wrote anything down, he just nodded and went on his way. Nevertheless, every time, he returned with the right drinks and dishes for everyone. Zeigarnik and Lewin were amazed at this impressive feat of memory. How did he do it? Would they, as highly educated individuals, have been able to flawlessly memorize the orders and serve them to the right people? No, they finally concluded. This man must be a genius!

© The Author(s) 2020
B. Kodden, *The Art of Sustainable Performance*, SpringerBriefs in Business,
https://doi.org/10.1007/978-3-030-46463-9_10

After everyone was finished eating and had left the restaurant, Bluma Zeigarnik realized that she had left her purse. She walked back and when she returned to the restaurant she greeted the waiter in question and asked him to help her find her purse. The waiter looked at her glazily. Who was she and where had she been sitting? He did not seem to have a clue. Zeigarnik was amazed, again. But this time for very different reasons. How could he not know? All night, the man had served her and her party without making a single mistake, never writing anything down. How could he have forgotten her face, just ten minutes after they had finished their dinner? What was going on here?

When asked how he could have forgotten her and her party so quickly, the waiter answered that he forgot all his orders as soon as he had delivered them to the table. And he forgot all about the check as soon as it had been settled. He apologized politely. His task had simply been completed and he had to fully shift his attention to the next task; new diners with new orders. He needed to completely shut himself off from everything but the orders that he was responsible for at that moment. That was the only way for him to do it. His uncompleted tasks were all that mattered!

Years of training and deliberate focus had given the waiter a memory that allowed him to flawlessly remember orders. Subconsciously and without writing anything down. He did not need to; his brain developed a system that easily processed orders. After they were paid, his mind would delete the bills in his head.

Zeigarnik and her mentor, the then already influential thinker Kurt Lewin, could not let this experience and the waiter's explanation go. They wondered if this phenomenon could be linked to a more general psychological principle. Do we all have a similar subconscious way to remember tasks yet to be completed? Could human memory make it possible to unconsciously distinguish between completed tasks and uncompleted tasks? (Zeigarnik 1927; Atkinson 1953; Baddeley 1963; Loflin 2014).

10.2   Memory Experiments

Zeigarnik decided to test the phenomenon using a large number of experiments in her laboratory. Her studies and hypotheses were confirmed, and the phenomenon of the use and possibilities of uncompleted tasks was born: The Zeigarnik effect. Once you know what you need to know and have a plan, a system, in place that you can first consciously and later subconsciously use, you can relax. You get into a flow, and you will have the unconscious competence to achieve sustainable performance. The Zeigarnik effect is the secret to the art of sustainable performance. Conscious, unconscious … competence!

The Zeigarnik effect is still very relevant today, even though so few people are aware of this phenomenon and the opportunities it offers. The Zeignarik effect and its theory show that uncompleted tasks keep going through our mind until the moment they are completed. Think of the waiter. As soon as the orders had been served and the party had settled up, he could cross them out.

Our brain will not let us rest before we can cross out these uncompleted tasks. Naturally, these tasks have to be relevant in order to be of use to us. After all, the Zeigarnik effect can also lead to negative results. For instance, think of all the messages popping up on your phone. Those are uncompleted tasks imposed on you by others (Heimbach and Jacoby 1972). More on that later.

10.3 A Plan Is Crucial

Over the years, there have been several theories (Atkinson 1953; Baddeley 1963; Heimbach and Jacoby 1972; Kiebel 2009; Loflin 2014) about how the Zeigarnik effect works, with two competing hypotheses dominating the debate. One theory said that the brain subconsciously tracks our goals so we can achieve them. That would mean that our random thoughts are actually a good sign; our subconsciousness remains vigilant until we achieve the goal.

Today, there is a different explanation for the Zeigarnik effect, which we have several recent experiments by Masicampo and Baumeister (2011) to thank for. Masicampo is a post-doctoral employee of the Florida State University who often works with Baumeister. For one of his studies, he had students think about how they were going to pass their most important upcoming exam. Half of the exam group got the assignment to make clear study plans indicating where and when they would study. However, during the experiments, nobody actually got to study. Instead, they were given a variety of other tasks. Afterwards, they were asked how well they had been able to focus and in what way their thoughts might have strayed.

The biggest difference the results showed was in the planning; a kind of unwritten cheat sheet. The participants who were asked to make a plan, a system, remained relatively focused. The students without a plan or system turned out to be stressed and they showed little focus on their main task, the exam. Despite what had been assumed for decades, the Zeigarnik effect turned out not to be a kind of alarm that keeps beeping until a task is completed. Rather, the subconscious mind urges the conscious mind to make a plan with details, a location, and circumstances. As soon as the plan was formed, the subconscious mind no longer had to bother the conscious mind by urging it, allowing one to relax (Masicampo and Baumeister 2011).

How great would it be if we—like Zeignarik's waiter—could develop a plan, a system, that could help us to complete our most important tasks. First consciously, later subconsciously, and eventually leading to sustainable performance? A "cheat sheet" that you would never have to look at because you know exactly what you have to do in order to make yourself, your team, or your organization successful again. This plan, this cheat sheet for sustainable performance, is what I want to hand to you with this study. As a professional, on what personality traits should you focus to remain winning? Which personality traits really matter when it comes to sustainable performance?

Our child prodigies did not turn into geniuses by accident. When it comes to self-management they often have one thing in common: The unconscious competence to apply the Zeigarnik effect. They set goals for themselves that matter and that suits who they are. They make a plan to achieve the goals, and cannot stop until the job is done. Then they can move on to the next goal, the next uncompleted task that will help them achieve their "why", their whakapapa. "To leave the jersey in a better place." They are able to gain unconscious competence. The highest stage of competence. Abraham Maslow

According to Maslow, there are four stages of learning, basically moving from unconscious awareness to conscious awareness. Maslow is most famous as a humanist psychology specialist. He developed a groundbreaking theory on human needs; Maslow's pyramid. Related to consciousness, competence, and learning phases, Abraham Maslow provided us with the following steps that will help us reach sustainable performance.

Stage 1: Unconscious Incompetence
Becoming consciously aware is one of the most important phases in the process towards sustainable performance. We are often not aware of our behavioral performance and its effects. We simply live our lives, without being aware of why we are not performing as well as we could. When that happens, you could consider yourself unconsciously incompetent. You react, act and behave as if you were on auto-pilot and do not understand why you keep running into the same issues. When you truly become aware of that, you can take back control of your life. That is when the Zeigarnik effect starts to develop. There are uncompleted tasks and goals waiting for you.

Stage 2: Conscious Incompetence
Once you realize that you have uncompleted tasks waiting for you and know that you are not doing what is needed to complete hem, you have become consciously incompetent. You understand that more is required in order to achieve your goals and sustainable performance, but you do not feel competent or able enough to do anything about it. For the first time, you are directly confronted by the often undesirable consequences of your current behavior. During this stage, you develop insight. Insight that has not yet been followed by action and a willingness to change. The Zeigarnik effect is born.

Stage 3: Conscious Incompetence
Changing, adapting, and pursuing new goals is a continuing process. Sustainable performance is like a lemniscate figure-eight symbol, going from thinking to doing, from action to reaction. Both poles need each other and keep each other balanced in order to fully develop. Lemniscate thinking is based on the idea that nothing exists without its counterpart. It is an ancient philosophy that can really help us think and act. There are many examples of contradictions like these. No happiness without misery. The same is true for sustainable performance. You first have to be unconsciously incompetent, before you can become unconsciously competent. By developing a plan, a system, that can help you compel your performance. Later, you might not even need the plan anymore; it will have become part of you.

Stage 4: Unconscious Competence

Once you are able to apply new behavior without consciously thinking about it, you have will have reached unconscious competence. You automatically use your new, more effective behavior. It almost becomes second nature. There will no longer be a difference between intent and result. You will be in full control. You will have embraced the Zeigarnik effect: The art of sustainable performance! (Maslow 1943).

10.4 Subconscious Ability

When I was reading the story about Bluma Zeigarnik's discovery, it hit me. What cheat sheet did I wish I had in order to improve myself as a person? What cheat sheet did I wish I had as an entrepreneur in order to surround myself with the best professionals who could help me elevate my business to a higher purpose? And what cheat sheet did I want to give to my young children in order to help them?

Billy Beane's story (Lewis 2003) and Bluma Zeigarnik's concept about unconsciously competent performance came together and inspired me to carry out my own study on performance indicators and personality traits—my very own *Moneyball*. All in order to use it for potentially creating a plan, a system that would enable us to develop ourselves and our organizations to a stage of sustainable performance.

The art of sustainable performance is achieving your highest goals—your most important uncompleted tasks—in an unconsciously competent way, by using a structured approach based on today's most important performance criteria and personality traits. Remember, (some) talent is good, (the right) character is everything. Personality traits such as self-efficacy and adaptability make all the difference!

What goals do you want to pursue? How can you increase your adaptability, self-efficacy, and work engagement? Create awareness of your uncompleted tasks. As soon as you are focused on goals that are truly important to you, your brain will compel you to action and urge you to make a plan. Once you have that plan, that system, you can let go without losing focus.

10.5 Letting Go Without Losing Focus

Many champions also use the Zeigarnik effect to achieve their outstanding performance at the right time. It enables them to let go of their tension before a game or match and focus completely on the unfinished task (Baumeister and Tierney 2012; Loflin 2014). One takes away the tension from the other. Take Usain Bolt, for example. Right before his most important competitions, he plays video games. He deliberately leaves the final game unfinished so his brain will make him think of that instead of the built-up tension for the Olympic final. Before I give a big presentation, I try to think about a Netflix show that I have not finished yet. Or about an upcoming long-distance run I am looking forward to. There are lots of uncompleted tasks we can think of to help us relax before we have to do something that makes us nervous.

I realized that I had not always competently used the Zeigarnik effect myself. I still do not always get it right today. Because the Zeigarnik effect also applies to uncompleted tasks that are far less important than our personal development or the performance of our teams or organizations. Consider your phone's screen lighting up when you receive an email, message, or tweet.

Your brain immediately wants to pay attention to it. It requires a certain ability to distinguish the importance of uncompleted tasks. So focus the Zeigarnik effect on your most important uncompleted tasks, your highest goals, your whakapapa. Discover and develop your crucial personality traits and learn to rely on the Zeigarnik effect. Engagement and sustainable performance will follow!

10.6   Recruitment and Selection

In order to strive for results, you need to select the right people. That much is clear. People with the right *mana,* as the All Blacks (Kerr 2013) say. Professionals with the right personality traits and performance indicators to perform, as Billy Beane might put it. People who strive for a collective goal, are engaged, can meet the mental and physical demands of their job, people who fit with the organization, and have the personality traits that are currently in demand. "Get the right people on the bus— you are the average of the people around you." Selecting the right people is the most important thing you need to be able to do as an entrepreneur, leader, HR professional, or team manager. The most important thing after *finding your goal,* that is (Collins 2001).

The All Blacks always start their selection process with the most important thing they strive for: *whakapapa*–the higher purpose. There is one goal that transcends all others. The All Blacks don't just want to win at the cost of everything else. On the contrary, it is about the execution, the pride, and the enthusiasm with which the right goals are pursued. All leading to that one purpose that they want to achieve: *to leave the black jersey in a better place.* The black jersey is a symbol of excellence, hard work, and individual and team sacrifice, all in order to become the best in the world.

When asked how the All Blacks selected the players for its team, former All Blacks coach Wayne Smith simply and clearly answered: "Talent was irrelevant. We carefully picked the players. We used *matrices* to back intuition because there are certain *stats* in rugby that determine a player's character. So we picked high work rate, strong body movers, and guys that were unselfish and had a sacrificial mindset." (Kerr 2013).

It is harder to hit closer to the inspiration for and results of my study than with the statement: "Talent is good, character is better." Intrinsic motivation, adaptability, and self-efficacy are the keys to sustainable performance. Look for the candidates who display these performance indicators the most, and ensure the right culture of performance using the right goals with the optimal Zeigarnik effect.

"To leave the jersey in a better place" is the ultimate example of a Zeigarnik effect. It is hard to imagine a more perfect uncompleted task. "The score takes care of itself."

References

Atkinson JW (1953) The achievement motive and recall of interrupted and completed tasks. J Exp Psychol 46(6):381–390

Baddeley AD (1963) A Zeigarnik-like effect in the recall of anagram solutions. Q J Exp Psychol 15(1):63–64

Baumeister RF, Tierney J (2012) Willpower. Why self-control is the secret to success

Collins J (2001) Good to great. Why some companies make the leap … and others don't. Harper Collins Publishers, New York, NY

Heimbach JT, Jacoby J (1972) The Zeigarnik effect in advertising. In: Proceedings of the third annual conference of the association of consumer research, pp 746–758

Kerr J (2013) Legacy. What the all blacks can teach us about the business of life. Constable and Robinson Ltd., London

Kiebel EM (2009) The effects of directed forgetting on completed and incompleted tasks. In: Presented at the 2nd annual student-faculty research celebration. Winona State University, Winona MN

Lewis M (2003) Moneyball. The art of winning an unfair game. Writers House, New York, NY

Loflin J (2014) Improving your productivity: the Zeigarnik effect. Consulted at: http://www.jonesloflin.com/jonesloflinblog/improving-your-productivity-the-Zeigarnik-effect/9222014

Masicampo EJ, Baumeister RF (2011) Consider it done! Plan making can eliminate the cognitive effects of unfulfilled goals. J Person Soci Psychol 101(4):667–683. Advance online publication. https://doi.org/10.1037/a0024192

Maslow AH (1943) A theory of human motivation. Psychol Rev 50(4):370–396. Consulted at: psychclassics.yorku.ca

Zeigarnik B (1927) Das BehalteneledigterundunerledigterHandlung. Psychologische Forschung 9:1–85

Conclusion and Summary

Abstract Why is it that some organizations manage to remain successful, whereas others break apart and disappear? Why are some people able to repeat their successes when nobody expected that they could? Why and based on what are certain talents hired in the Netherlands, while others are rejected? And do we perhaps all have the same blind spot when it comes to finding the right employee?

Keywords Selection criteria · Personality traits · Professional development · Sustainable performance

Introduction

My study, as well as studies by many others, including Schmidt and Hunter (1998), Randstad, and the University of Amsterdam (2008), show that our knowledge about sustainable performance and the use of performance and selection criteria are wholly inadequate. I believe many Dutch organizations urgently need a new perspective on talent and performance management to achieve sustainable performance. A perspective that is based on the idea that "talent is good, character is better!"

Supervisors and HR specialists should look closer at the character of candidates. At their mental abilities, their specific personality traits, and their sustainable employability. How many professionals are not even being given the right opportunities to make the most of their talents? Professionals that might not have the right degrees or experience yet, but who are prepared to give anything to succeed and gain the necessary skills and knowledge. This is not just a missed opportunity for professionals and organizations, but for the Netherlands as a whole. Developing and creating opportunities for professionals who have what it takes is something that concerns us all.

With this book, I wanted to hand you a plan, a system to achieve sustainable performance, using five themes. A model that could be used and applied by professionals as well as organizations.

I started the book discussing literature about the importance of sustainable performance, using the *kiss of death* metaphor. Winning once is not good enough! The second theme of sustainable performance related to the idea that numbers tell the tale. Through the stories of Billy Beane and *Moneyball*, (Lewis 2003) this led to the start of my own research. The third theme of sustainable performance, the importance of several suggested and studied performance criteria and personality traits, can be found in Chaps. 1 through 8. In Chap. 9, I discussed the importance of a strong performance culture using the story of the best performing organization in recent decades, the All Blacks.

In Chap. 10, I used the Zeigarnik effect—and the results of studies by Baumeister and Tierney 2012) and Maiscampo (2011) and others—to explain how you can create a plan to combine these themes into the highest form of execution; unconscious competence. Through these five themes, my definition of the art of sustainable performance emerged.

In an unconsciously competent way (1), realize (2) your highest goals—your most important uncompleted tasks (3) by creating a plan (4) based on the most important performance criteria and personality traits (5).

Professional Development

In the box and Fig. 1, you can find the framework showing the most important personality traits and performance criteria according to this study.

The most important personality traits according to this study are self-efficacy (number 1 overall), adaptability (2), intrinsic motivation (4), and intelligence (5). The most important aspects of work dedication are dedication (6) and vigor (7). Furthermore, the most important element of organizational fit is the fit with the supervisor. The most important elements of the fit with the job requirements are the mental requirements (3). Talent itself can be found in the 9th place on the overall list.

Doing what you are good at, continually adapting yourself and your organizations to new circumstances, taking care of your physical and mental fitness to be able to meet the mental job requirements; my study has shown that these traits are the main criteria for success.

The five necessary traits of professionals who have achieved sustainable performance are as follows:

1. Know and believe in your strengths, focus on them (*self-efficacy*).
2. Develop a strong adaptive ability and use it to take on the challenges and opportunities of tomorrow (*adaptability*).
3. Be vigorous and aware of the mental job requirements that are asked of you (*vigor/fit with mental job requirements*).
4. Ensure that you are intrinsically motivated for your job.
    –ensure a high level of education (*intrinsic motivation/dedication*).
5. Acknowledge the value of the talent. Talent is overrated, but we cannot ignore it completely. Make sure you are on the right podium (*talent/organizational fit*).

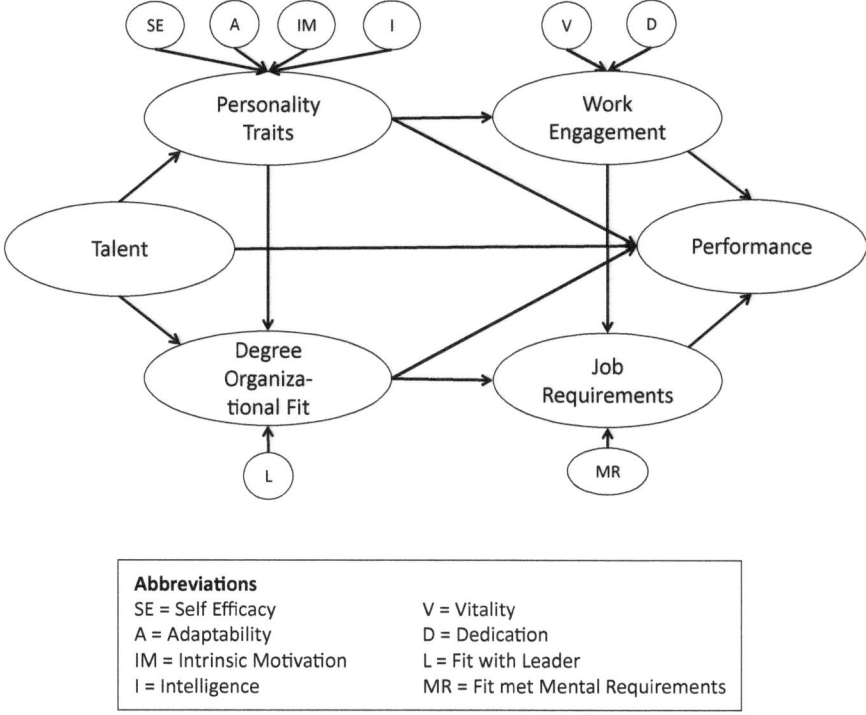

Fig. 1 Framework for sustainable professional development (from talent to performance)

So then, is talent completely unnecessary? The level of talent present in a candidate did turn out to have a positive correlation to performance but did sufficiently explain the range of performance levels. It ended the 9th of the 21 performance criteria included in this study. This result matches that of many studies on child prodigies and the importance of talent; talent is (seriously) overrated.

Organizational Development

The research model can also be used by organizations to recruit and select candidates. The left part of the model is about vital personality traits and organizational fit. The right part is about the assessment criteria for when the professional is on board. By hiring employees based on important personality traits such as self-efficacy, adaptability, intelligence, and intrinsic motivation plus organizational fit, and later by selecting on the basis of proven work engagement, mental fit with the job requirements and achieved results, the chance of sustainable performance increases.

From my study of supervisors and senior colleagues of over 1100 professionals (which took place between 2014 and 2016), self-efficacy, adaptability, intrinsic

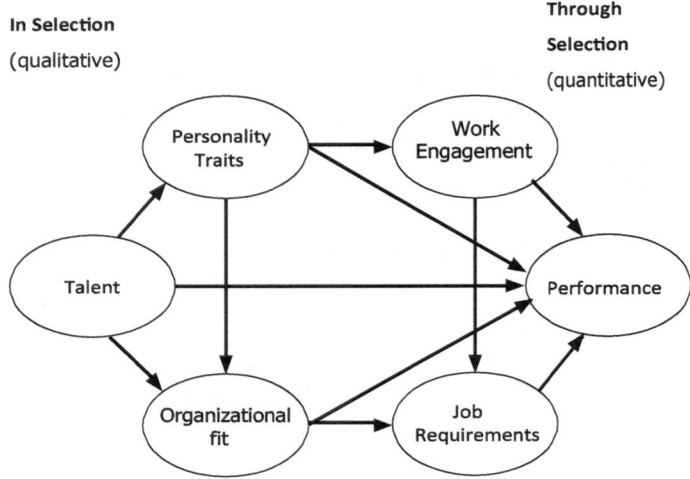

Fig. 2 Framework for recruitment and selection

motivation, and intelligence emerged as the most important personality traits for sustainable performance. As mentioned earlier, these results need to be considered with a certain level of skepticism.

Beware: Despite the fact that the sample test had three times the required number of respondents, any study—including mine—has its limitations and can be susceptible to bias and socially desirable responses. In addition, the study was carried out cross-sectionally, which means that it is possible that different results may have emerged at later times. The outcomes of this study are therefore solely meant to be taken as a guideline. In addition, certain personality traits and/or performance criteria should be given less or extra weight, depending on the profession, industry, and situation. The framework in Fig. 2 and the list of performance indicators (see page 38) can be used to design your own recruitment and selection model.

My study demonstrated that you can increase the chance for sustainable performance by recruiting and hiring employees using semi-structured interviews and looking for the following indicators: self-efficacy, adaptability, and intrinsic motivation (see the questionnaires provided in the tools section). Moreover, it is also recommended to have the candidate take an intelligence test and to estimate the fit with the supervisor. Always consider talent as a conditional element for the position. You can find the completed framework for recruitment and selection in Fig. 3—Model for Recruitment and Selection.

After some time, for instance, after a long trial or training period, you can determine yourself whether these criteria can be expanded upon and assessed quantitatively using vital performance indicators such as work engagement and its elements of vigor and dedication. In addition, also assess the proven fit with the mental job requirements. The criteria should be linked to both past and future performance.

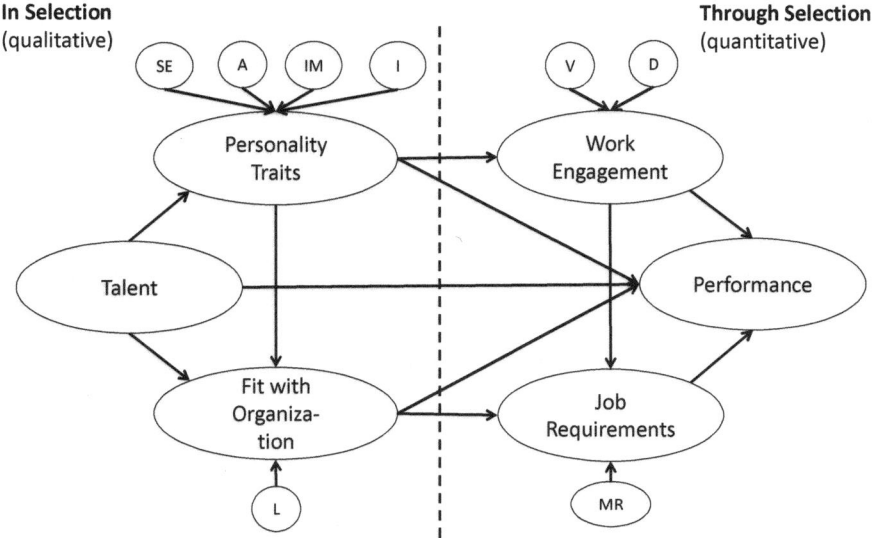

Fig. 3 Model for recruitment and selection

By monitoring employees over a longer period of time (longitudinal) and assessing them using the most important performance indicators (as shown by this study), sustainable performance can be achieved *and* maintained. Do consider that, in addition to hiring and keeping the right employees, this requires two more Ps. These are providing a sense of meaning (Purpose) and safeguarding the right norms and values(Principles). Purpose, People, Principles. Or as the All Blacks have taught us (Kerr 2013): whakapapa, mana, ubuntu. With the addition of the Ps Passion (haka) and Partnership (whanau), we have all five traits of organizations that achieve sustainable performance.

The Five Traits (5 Ps)of Organizations that Achieve Sustainable Performance are as follows:

1. *People* (mana): Select the right people to strive for this goal—"talent is good, character is better"(P1).
2. *Purpose* (whakapapa): Create an inspiring uncompleted task, a "why": a higher purpose => the Zeigarnik-effect! (P2).
3. *Principles* (ubuntu): Develop and maintain a strong organizational culture, based on the right principles(P3).
4. *Passion* (haka): Encourage sustainable performance by continually focusing on leadership, energy, and inspiration (P4).
5. *Partnership* (whanau): Ensure that employees feel common ownership of and connection to the desired result (P5).

References

Baumeister RF, Tierney J (2012) Willpower. Why self-control is the secret to success.

Kerr J (2013) Legacy. What the all blacks can teach us about the business of life. Constable & Robinson Ltd., London

Lewis M (2003) Moneyball. The art of winning an unfair game. Writers House, New York, NY

Masicampo EJ, Baumeister RF (2011) Consider it done! Plan making can eliminate the cognitive effects of unfulfilled goals. J Personal Soc Psychol 101(4):667–683. Advance online publication. doi: 10.1037/a0024192

Schmidt F, Hunter J (1998) The validity and utility of selection methods in personnel psychology: practical and theoretical implications of 85 years of research findings. Psychol Bull 124(2):262–274.

UvA (2008) Personeelsselectie in tijden van krapte. Onderzoek door UvA en Randstad, Diemen.

Appendix A
Justification of the Study

A validated study of a target group like the one that was used here requires 384 respondents on scientific grounds (see explanation below). However, I decided that to have a better foundation for any conclusions, I should triple this number.

Respondents

As I have indicated before, the study was done among senior colleagues and supervisors of over 1100 professionals. These people worked in a variety of sectors of the services industry in the Netherlands between 2014 and 2016. Although the number 1,100 might appear random, it did, in fact, have a background and a reason. The respondents were participants of leadership programs inside and outside of Nyenrode Business University. All were in a position of seniority, which enabled them to provide valuable remarks on the sustainable performance of the professionals they worked with. In order to limit bias and politically correct responses, the supervisors and senior colleagues were asked to randomly and anonymously pick the professionals they would evaluate. These could be professionals who performed excellently, as well as professionals with less impressive performance levels. The names and positions of the professionals in question were never known to the researcher and others. This approach limited the risk of bias and politically correct responses as much as possible.

Sample Size

Calculating and determining the sample size can be quite challenging because it involves complicated formulas. The required sample size is mostly determined by the size of the population, the desired reliability, the accuracy, and the margin for error with which realistic conclusions can be drawn. Below you will find respective explanations of these concepts.

Population

The population size is the same as the answer to the following question: how many people are there in the total target group? It is possible that the population size is unknown. In that case, one could use the number 20,000, since the sample size does

© The Editor(s) (if applicable) and The Author(s) 2020
B. Kodden, *The Art of Sustainable Performance*, SpringerBriefs in Business,
https://doi.org/10.1007/978-3-030-46463-9

not change much for populations larger than 20,000. For my study on professionals, I used students and participants of leadership programs. Respondents were people who had degrees like a Master's of Business or a Master's of Science in Business Administration. Well-educated, usually supervising and senior employees, who were asked to fill out the performance indicators for anonymously and randomly chosen close colleagues. Almost three out of ten in the 15–75 age group in the Netherlands are at least college-educated. Not all of those currently work as professionals, of course. According to the Dutch statistics bureau, there are currently seven million people employed in the Netherlands (not just in the services industry this study focused on). A population size of one million was used (among other factors) to determine the sample size for this study. As stated earlier though, the sample size does not change significantly for population sizes greater than 20,000.

Reliability

In practice, market research agencies use various reliability percentages to calculate the sample size. Often, statements are based on 95%. That means that the results of the study will be the same in 19 out of 20 cases. Other, less frequently used reliability percentages are 90 and 99%. This study used a reliability percentage of 95%.

Accuracy

Any study based on a sample test will deviate from reality to a certain extent. This deviation is the sample test margin for error or accuracy. It depends on the sample size and the percentage result of the study. Generally speaking, the larger the sample size, the lower the accuracy margin, and the closer the percentage is to 50%, the higher the accuracy margin.

For example: for a sample size of $n = 100$, the maximum accuracy margin is 9.8%. That means that if a result of the study is that 50% of the respondents are male, the actual percentage of males in the population is between 40.2 and 59.8%. If the percentage result is for instance 10% however, the accuracy margin is only 5.9%. That means that if the study shows that 10% is male, the actual percentage in the population lies somewhere between 4.1 and 15.9%. After determining the desired sample size, it is common to assume a result of 50%. This percentage has the largest margin for accuracy. In general, studies often use sample sizes with a maximum accuracy deviation of 5% is. The same was true for this study.

For a study like this, in which the results need to be able to be generalized to all professionals working in Dutch service industries, and with the desired accuracy of 5% and reliability of 95%, the sample size would need to be 384 respondents.

Research Model

So which personality traits are important for sustainable performance by professionals? And how can performance criteria be linked? Based on literature and the results of other studies, the following research model emerged: (Fig. A.1)

Using this research model, I decided to ask over 1,100 senior colleagues and supervisors to evaluate a particular colleague or employee based on questions like: "This employee has above-average intrinsic motivation to excel."; Compared to his/her

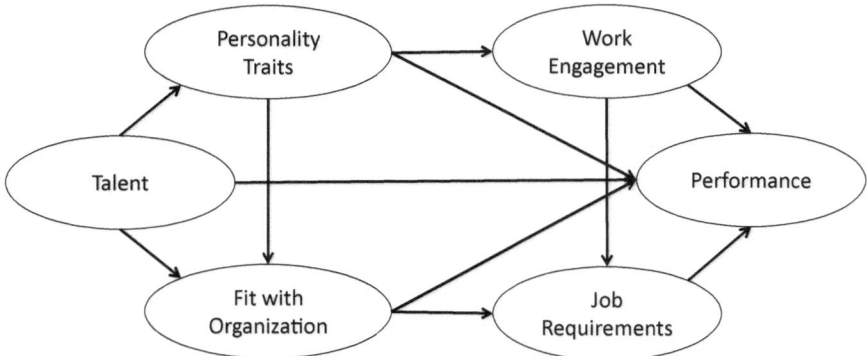

Fig. A.1 Research model

colleagues, this employee has, on average, much less/less/neutral/more/much more natural talent and innate aptitude to excel in his/her profession. "This employee shows above-average confidence in difficult situations." With possible answers like "completely agree, agree, neutral, disagree, and completely disagree." In this way, a total of over 1100 professionals were evaluated on their level of talent for their job, the extent to which they matched the twelve personal traits, the three aspects of work engagement, three aspects of organizational fit, the extent to which they were able to meet the mental and physical job requirements, and their individual and team performance of the last five. The five concepts that were charted using this approach were as follows:

- The level of talent for their job;
- the level of specific personality traits;
- the level of organizational fit;
- the level of work engagement;
- the level of fit with the (mental and physical) job requirements.

These elements were then linked to the level of sustainable performance by professionals, both as individuals and as part of a team.

Hypotheses

The goal of the study was to test several hypotheses. In order to test these hypotheses, the contributing variables first needed to be tested for normalcy, reliability, and internal consistency by carrying out several factor analyses and calculating, among others, Cronbach's alpha and KMO scores. The Cronbach's alpha scores of all variables were between 0.711 and 0.861. These scores can be interpreted as amply sufficient to very good. The KMO scores of all variables were between 0.500 and 0.883, which can be considered acceptable to very acceptable.

After carrying out these preliminary tests, the various correlation and (multiple) regression analyses could be carried out to test the hypotheses and measure the importance of the different variables and contributed personality traits.

The research model itself was tested using Structural Equation Modeling with the AMOS program. The various analyses and tables can be found in the following appendices.

Appendix B
Important Results of the Study on Performance Indicators

Explained variation (beta) for performance (significance):

1. Level of self-efficacy = 0.198(0.000)
2. Level of adaptability = 0.161(0.000)
3. Fit with mental job requirements = 0.153(0.000)
4. Intrinsic motivation 0.089(0.004)
5. Intelligence = 0.060(0.016)
6. Dedication = 0.056(0.039)
7. Vigor = 0.050(0.060)
8. Fit with physical job requirements = 0.041(0.090)
9. Talent = 0.049(0.094)
10. Extrinsic motivation =0.034(0.099)

Item 1–4: significant < 0.005
Item 5–6: significant < 0.05
Item 7–10: significant < 0.1
*No significant correlation was found for the other items.

© The Editor(s) (if applicable) and The Author(s) 2020
B. Kodden, *The Art of Sustainable Performance*, SpringerBriefs in Business,
https://doi.org/10.1007/978-3-030-46463-9

Appendix C
Correlation Matrix

See Table C.1.

Table C.1 Correlation matrix

Correlations		Talent	Willpower	Self-preservation	Intrinsic motivation	Extrinsic motivation	Optimism	Stubborn	Stress resistant	Self-efficacy	Adaptability
Talent	Pearson Correlation	1	0.540**	0.482**	0.529**	0.124**	0.335**	0.308**	0.431**	0.567**	0.474**
	Sig. (2-tailed)		0.000	0.000	0.000	0.000	0.000	0.000	0.000	0.000	0.000
Will	Pearson Correlation	0.540**	1	0.414**	0.677**	0.210**	0.346**	0.275**	0.335**	0.455**	0.414**
	Sig. (2-tailed)	0.000		0.000	0.000	0.000	0.000	0.000	0.000	0.000	0.000
Self-control	Pearson Correlation	0.482**	0.414**	1	0.440**	0.081*	0.339**	0.206**	0.410**	0.477**	0.411**
	Sig. (2-tailed)	0.000	0.000		0.000	0.013	0.000	0.000	0.000	0.000	0.000
Intrinsic motivation	Pearson correlation	0.529**	0.677**	0.440**	1	0.097**	0.389**	0.248**	0.342**	0.491**	0.461**
	Sig. (2-tailed)	0.000	0.000	0.000		0.003	0.000	0.000	0.000	0.000	0.000
Extrinsic motivation	Pearson correlation	0.124**	0.210**	0.081*	0.097**	1	0.110**	0.146**	0.072*	0.049	0.120**
	Sig. (2-tailed)	0.000	0.000	0.013	0.003		0.001	0.000	0.028	0.137	0.000
Optimism	Pearson correlation	0.335**	0.346**	0.339**	0.389**	0.110**	1	0.403**	0.442**	0.349**	0.479**
	Sig. (2-tailed)	0.000	0.000	0.000	0.000	0.001		0.000	0.000	0.000	0.000

(continued)

Table C.1 (continued)

Correlations		Talent	Willpower	Self-preservation	Intrinsic motivation	Extrinsic motivation	Optimism	Stubborn	Stress resistant	Self-efficacy	Adaptability
Self-esteem	Pearson correlation	0.308**	0.275**	0.206**	0.248**	0.146**	0.403**	1	0.445**	0.265**	0.280**
	Sig. (2-tailed)	0.000	0.000	0.000	0.000	0.000	0.000		0.000	0.000	0.000
Stress resistant	Pearson correlation	0.431**	0.335**	0.410**	0.342**	0.072*	0.442**	0.445**	1	0.536**	0.449**
	Sig. (2-tailed)	0.000	0.000	0.000	0.000	0.028	0.000	0.000		0.000	0.000
Self-efficacy	Pearson correlation	0.567**	0.455**	0.477**	0.491**	0.049	0.349**	0.265**	0.536**	1	0.581**
	Sig. (2-tailed)	0.000	0.000	0.000	0.000	0.137	0.000	0.000	0.000		0.000
Adaptability	Pearson correlation	0.474**	0.414**	0.411**	0.461**	0.120**	0.479**	0.280**	0.449**	0.581**	1
	Sig. (2-tailed)	0.000	0.000	0.000	0.000	0.000	0.000	0.000	0.000	0.000	
Self-confidence	Pearson correlation	0.497**	0.392**	0.355**	0.351**	0.187**	0.394**	0.499**	0.588**	0.484**	0.469**
	Sig. (2-tailed)	0.000	0.000	0.000	0.000	0.000	0.000	0.000	0.000	0.000	0.000
Intelligence	Pearson correlation	0.559**	0.369**	0.386**	0.390**	0.104**	0.264**	0.243**	0.374**	0.444**	0.407**
	Sig. (2-tailed)	0.000	0.000	0.000	0.000	0.002	0.000	0.000	0.000	0.000	0.000

(continued)

Table C.1 (continued)

Correlations		Talent	Willpower	Self-preservation	Intrinsic motivation	Extrinsic motivation	Optimism	Stubborn	Stress resistant	Self-efficacy	Adaptability
Vigor	Pearson correlation	0.454**	0.483**	0.324**	0.517**	0.106**	0.464**	0.339**	0.459**	0.442**	0.471**
	Sig. (2-tailed)	0.000	0.000	0.000	0.000	0.001	0.000	0.000	0.000	0.000	0.000
Dedication	Pearson correlation	0.396**	0.512**	0.321**	0.582**	0.029	0.390**	0.224**	0.345**	0.409**	0.396**
	Sig. (2-tailed)	0.000	0.000	0.000	0.000	0.373	0.000	0.000	0.000	0.000	0.000
Absorption	Pearson correlation	0.428**	0.466**	0.376**	0.529**	0.085**	0.277**	0.211**	0.309**	0.427**	0.398**
	Sig. (2-tailed)	0.000	0.000	0.000	0.000	0.010	0.000	0.000	0.000	0.000	0.000
Fit with job	Pearson correlation	0.533**	0.405**	0.446**	0.470**	0.066*	0.321**	0.240**	0.395**	0.544**	0.496**
	Sig. (2-tailed)	0.000	0.000	0.000	0.000	0.044	0.000	0.000	0.000	0.000	0.000
Fit with culture	Pearson correlation	0.377**	0.321**	0.305**	0.388**	0.074*	0.342**	0.181**	0.276**	0.391**	0.446**
	Sig. (2-tailed)	0.000	0.000	0.000	0.000	0.023	0.000	0.000	0.000	0.000	0.000
Fit with leadership style	Pearson correlation	0.275**	0.242**	0.245**	0.290**	0.095**	0.277**	0.180**	0.257**	0.358**	0.375**
	Sig. (2-tailed)	0.000	0.000	0.000	0.000	0.004	0.000	0.000	0.000	0.000	0.000

(continued)

Table C.1 (continued)

Correlations		Talent	Willpower	Self-preservation	Intrinsic motivation	Extrinsic motivation	Optimism	Stubborn	Stress resistant	Self-efficacy	Adaptability
Physical job requirements	Pearson correlation	0.380**	0.318**	0.297**	0.358**	0.121**	0.305**	0.262**	0.380**	0.387**	0.361**
	Sig. (2-tailed)	0.000	0.000	0.000	0.000	0.000	0.000	0.000	0.000	0.000	0.000
Mental job requirements	Pearson correlation	0.553**	0.428**	0.450**	0.456**	0.100**	0.386**	0.335**	0.527**	0.565**	0.533**
	Sig. (2-tailed)	0.000	0.000	0.000	0.000	0.002	0.000	0.000	0.000	0.000	0.000
Personal performance	Pearson correlation	0.520**	0.474**	0.437**	0.493**	0.121**	0.350**	0.268**	0.384**	0.587**	0.524**
	Sig. (2-tailed)	0.000	0.000	0.000	0.000	0.000	0.000	0.000	0.000	0.000	0.000
Speed performance	Pearson correlation	0.478**	0.442**	0.376**	0.453**	0.179**	0.318**	0.279**	0.387**	0.532**	0.497**
	Sig. (2-tailed)	0.000	0.000	0.000	0.000	0.000	0.000	0.000	0.000	0.000	0.000
Contribution team performance	Pearson correlation	0.553**	0.464**	0.439**	0.562**	0.058	0.424**	0.244**	0.429**	0.611**	0.594**
	Sig. (2-tailed)	0.000	0.000	0.000	0.000	0.077	0.000	0.000	0.000	0.000	0.000

*Correlation is significant at the 0.05 level (2-tailed) **Correlation is significant at the 0.01 level (2-tailed)

	Self-confidence	Intelligence	Vigor	Dedication	Absorption	Fit with job	Fit with culture	Fit with supervisor	Physical job requirements	Mental job requirements	Personal performance	Speed performance	Team performance
	0.497**	0.559**	0.454**	0.396**	0.428**	0.533**	0.377**	0.275**	0.380**	0.553**	0.520**	0.478**	0.553**
	0.000	0.000	0.000	0.000	0.000	0.000	0.000	0.000	0.000	0.000	0.000	0.000	0.000
	0.392**	0.369**	0.483**	0.512**	0.466**	0.405**	0.321**	0.242**	0.318**	0.428**	0.474**	0.442**	0.464**
	0.000	0.000	0.000	0.000	0.000	0.000	0.000	0.000	0.000	0.000	0.000	0.000	0.000
	0.355**	0.386**	0.324**	0.321**	0.376**	0.446**	0.305**	0.245**	0.297**	0.450**	0.437**	0.376**	0.439**
	0.000	0.000	0.000	0.000	0.000	0.000	0.000	0.000	0.000	0.000	0.000	0.000	0.000
	0.351**	0.390**	0.517**	0.582**	0.529**	0.470**	0.388**	0.290**	0.358**	0.456**	0.493**	0.453**	0.562**
	0.000	0.000	0.000	0.000	0.000	0.000	0.000	0.000	0.000	0.000	0.000	0.000	0.000
	0.187**	0.104**	0.106**	0.029	0.085**	0.066*	0.074*	0.095**	0.121**	0.100**	0.121**	0.179**	0.058
	0.000	0.002	0.001	0.373	0.01	0.044	0.023	0.004	0.000	0.002	0.000	0.000	0.077
	0.394**	0.264**	0.464**	0.390**	0.277**	0.321**	0.342**	0.277**	0.305**	0.386**	0.350**	0.318**	0.424**
	0.000	0.000	0.000	0.000	0.000	0.000	0.000	0.000	0.000	0.000	0.000	0.000	0.000
	0.499**	0.243**	0.339**	0.224**	0.211**	0.240**	0.181**	0.180**	0.262**	0.335**	0.268**	0.279**	0.244**
	0.000	0.000	0.000	0.000	0.000	0.000	0.000	0.000	0.000	0.000	0.000	0.000	0.000
	0.588**	0.374**	0.459**	0.345**	0.309**	0.395**	0.276**	0.257**	0.380**	0.527**	0.384**	0.387**	0.429**
	0.000	0.000	0.000	0.000	0.000	0.000	0.000	0.000	0.000	0.000	0.000	0.000	0.000
	0.484**	0.444**	0.442**	0.409**	0.427**	0.544**	0.391**	0.358**	0.387**	0.565**	0.587**	0.532**	0.611**
	0.000	0.000	0.000	0.000	0.000	0.000	0.000	0.000	0.000	0.000	0.000	0.000	0.000
	0.469**	0.407**	0.471**	0.396**	0.398**	0.496**	0.446**	0.375**	0.361**	0.533**	0.524**	0.497**	0.594**
	0.000	0.000	0.000	0.000	0.000	0.000	0.000	0.000	0.000	0.000	0.000	0.000	0.000
	1	0.431**	0.403**	0.324**	0.343**	0.409**	0.277**	0.262**	0.351**	0.516**	0.408**	0.434**	0.412**
		0.000	0.000	0.000	0.000	0.000	0.000	0.000	0.000	0.000	0.000	0.000	0.000
	0.431**	1	0.385**	0.281**	0.345**	0.394**	0.273**	0.178**	0.328**	0.502**	0.428**	0.440**	0.412**
	0.000		0.000	0.000	0.000	0.000	0.000	0.000	0.000	0.000	0.000	0.000	0.000
	0.403**	0.385**	1	0.502**	0.422**	0.416**	0.338**	0.259**	0.472**	0.471**	0.449**	0.465**	0.483**
				0.000	0.000	0.000	0.000	0.000	0.000	0.000	0.000	0.000	0.000

(continued)

(continued)

	Self-confidence	Intelligence	Vigor	Dedication	Absorption	Fit with job	Fit with culture	Fit with supervisor	Physical job requirements	Mental job requirements	Personal performance	Speed performance	Team performance
Dedication	0.324**	0.281**	0.502**	1	0.503**	0.407**	0.459**	0.311**	0.311**	0.374**	0.396**	0.369**	0.517**
	0.000	0.000	0.000		0.000	0.000	0.000	0.000	0.000	0.000	0.000	0.000	0.000
Absorption	0.343**	0.345**	0.422**	0.503**	1	0.453**	0.325**	0.236**	0.303**	0.406**	0.413**	0.416**	0.441**
	0.000	0.000	0.000	0.000		0.000	0.000	0.000	0.000	0.000	0.000	0.000	0.000
Fit with job	0.409**	0.394**	0.416**	0.407**	0.453**	1	0.518**	0.385**	0.397**	0.527**	0.502**	0.471**	0.561**
	0.000	0.000	0.000	0.000	0.000		0.000	0.000	0.000	0.000	0.000	0.000	0.000
Fit with culture	0.277**	0.273**	0.338**	0.459**	0.325**	0.518**	1	0.564**	0.300**	0.361**	0.376**	0.348**	0.466**
	0.000	0.000	0.000	0.000	0.000	0.000		0.000	0.000	0.000	0.000	0.000	0.000
Fit with supervisor	0.262**	0.178**	0.259**	0.311**	0.236**	0.385**	0.564**	1	0.285**	0.348**	0.366**	0.312**	0.363**
	0.000	0.000	0.000	0.000	0.000	0.000	0.000		0.000	0.000	0.000	0.000	0.000
Physical job requirements	0.351**	0.328**	0.472**	0.311**	0.303**	0.397**	0.300**	0.285**	1	0.552**	0.408**	0.399**	0.409**
	0.000	0.000	0.000	0.000	0.000	0.000	0.000	0.000		0.000	0.000	0.000	0.000
Mental job requirements	0.516**	0.502**	0.471**	0.374**	0.406**	0.527**	0.361**	0.348**	0.552**	1	0.575**	0.544**	0.556**
	0.000	0.000	0.000	0.000	0.000	0.000	0.000	0.000	0.000		0.000	0.000	0.000
Personal performance	0.408**	0.428**	0.449**	0.396**	0.413**	0.502**	0.376**	0.366**	0.408**	0.575**	1	0.711**	0.583**
	0.000	0.000	0.000	0.000	0.000	0.000	0.000	0.000	0.000	0.000		0.000	0.000
Speed performance	0.434**	0.440**	0.465**	0.369**	0.416**	0.471**	0.348**	0.312**	0.399**	0.544**	0.711**	1	0.559**
	0.000	0.000	0.000	0.000	0.000	0.000	0.000	0.000	0.000	0.000	0.000		0.000
Team performance	0.412**	0.412**	0.483**	0.517**	0.441**	0.561**	0.466**	0.363**	0.409**	0.556**	0.583**	0.559**	1
	0.000	0.000	0.000	0.000	0.000	0.000	0.000	0.000	0.000	0.000	0.000	0.000	

Appendix D
Correlation Matrix Factors

See Table D.1.

© The Editor(s) (if applicable) and The Author(s) 2020
B. Kodden, *The Art of Sustainable Performance*, SpringerBriefs in Business,
https://doi.org/10.1007/978-3-030-46463-9

Table D.1 Correlation matrix factors

		Talent	Personality traits	Work engagement	Organizational fit	Job requirements	Performance
Talent	Pearson correlation	1	0.688**	0.529**	0.368**	0.533**	0.601**
	Sig. (2-tailed)		0	0	0	0	0
	N	1122	1122	1122	1122	1122	1122
Personality traits	Pearson correlation	0.688**	1	0.681**	0.512**	0.646**	0.769**
	Sig. (2-tailed)	0		0	0	0	0
	N	1122	1122	1122	1122	1122	1122
Work engagement	Pearson correlation	0.529**	0.681**	1	0.447**	0.548**	0.632**
	Sig. (2-tailed)	0	0		0	0	0
	N	1122	1122	1122	1122	1122	1122
Organizational fit	Pearson correlation	0.368**	0.512**	0.447***	1	0.416**	0.488**
	Sig. (2-tailed)	0	0	0		0	0
	N	1122	1122	1122	1122	1122	1122
Job requirements	Pearson correlation	0.533**	0.646**	0.548***	0.416**	1	0.638**
	Sig. (2-tailed)	0	0	0	0		0
	N	1122	1122	1122	1122	1122	1122
Performance	Pearson correlation	0.601**	0.769**	0.632**	0.488**	0.638**	1
	Sig. (2-tailed)	0	0	0	0	0	
	N	1122	1122	1122	1122	1122	1122

*Correlation is significant at the 0.05 level (2-tailed)
**Correlation is significant at the 0.01 level (2-tailed)

Appendix E
Regression Analysis

See Table E.1.

Table E.1 Regression analysis

Model		Unstandardized coefficients		Standardized coefficients	t	Sig.
		B	Std. Error	Beta		
1	(Constant)	−0.05	0.108		−0.466	0.641
	Willpower	0.037	0.024	0.046	1.582	0.114
	Self-control	0.027	0.022	0.029	1.192	0.234
	Intrinsic motivation	0.072	0.025	0.089	2.917	0.004
	Extrinsic motivation	0.031	0.019	0.034	1.652	0.099
	Optimism	0.013	0.021	0.016	0.632	0.528
	Self-esteem	−0.013	0.021	−0.015	−0.612	0.541
	Stress resistant	−0.017	0.023	−0.021	−0.742	0.458
	Self-efficacy	0.165	0.024	0.198	6.83	0
	Adaptability	0.13	0.022	0.161	5.795	0
	Self-confidence	0.008	0.022	0.01	0.376	0.707
	Intelligence	0.052	0.022	0.06	2.404	0.016
	Vigor	0.043	0.023	0.05	1.884	0.06
	Dedication	0.048	0.023	0.056	2.063	0.039
	Absorption	0.026	0.018	0.035	1.402	0.161
	Fit with culture	0.022	0.024	0.025	0.896	0.371
	Fit with supervisor style	0.027	0.021	0.031	1.286	0.199
	Physical job requirements	0.041	0.024	0.041	1.696	0.09

(continued)

Table E.1 (continued)

Model	Unstandardized coefficients		Standardized coefficients	t	Sig.
	B	Std. Error	Beta		
Mental job requirements	0.144	0.028	0.153	5.157	0
Talent	0.05	0.03	0.049	1.679	0.094

Appendix F
Results of Study on the Use of Selection Criteria

Among over fifty CEOs of large and publicly traded companies

- Talent
- Intrinsic motivation
- Intelligence
- Fit with organizational culture
- Self-confidence
- Dedication
- Wilpower
- Ambition
- Stress resistance
- Self-efficacy
- Vigor
- Adaptability
- Absorption
- Fit with job
- Optimism

Appendix G
Results of Study on Pad-Analysis and Fit Research Model (Structural Equation Modeling)

Minimum was achieved
Chi-square = 35.006
Degrees of freedom = 2
Probability level = 0.000 (Table G.1; Fig. G.1).

Table G.1 Research model analysis—pad analysis (AMOS)

		Estimate	SE	CR	P	Label
Personal traits	Talent	0.663	0.021	30.866	***	par_1
Organizational fit	Talent	0.001	0.046	0.021	0.983	par_4
Organizational fit	Personality traits	0.487	0.049	9.884	***	par_10
Work engagement	Personality traits	0.669	0.028	24.104	***	par_2
Work engagement	Organizational fit	0.076	0.022	3.435	***	par_8
Job requirements	Organizational fit	0.083	0.022	3.678	***	par_3
Job requirements	Personal traits	0.677	0.035	19.155	***	par_9
Job requirements	Work engagement	0.077	0.031	2.493	0.013	par_11
Performance	Work engagement	0.130	0.023	5.574	***	par_5
Performance	Job requirements	0.177	0.023	7.639	***	par_6
Performance	Talent	0.080	0.026	3.103	0.002	par_7
Performance	Personal traits	0.504	0.037	13.497	***	par_12
Performance	Organizational fit	0.072	0.017	4.237	***	par_13

***Correlation is significant at the 0.001 level (2-tailed)

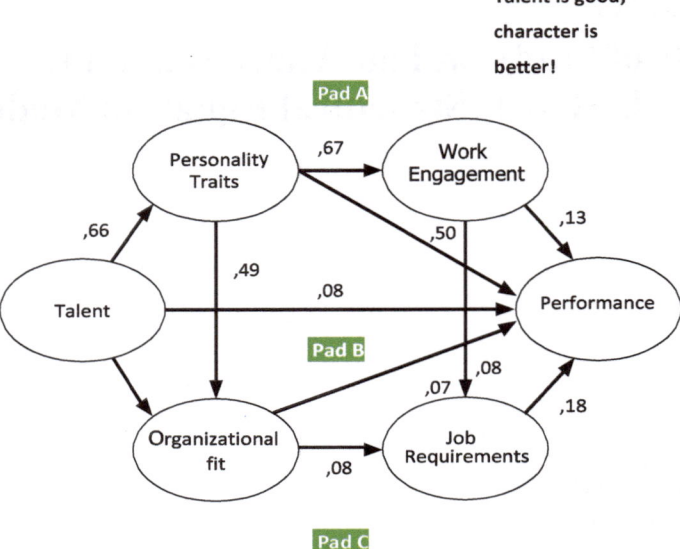

Fig. G.1 Pad-analysis research model "talent is good, character is better"

Appendix H
Research Model Analysis—Model-Fit Analysis (AMOS)

See Table H.1.

Table H.1 Research model analysis—model-fit analysis (AMOS)

Baseline comparisons					
Model	NFI	RFI	IFI	TLI	CFI
	Delta1	rho1	Delta2	rho2	
Default model	0.989	0.885	0.990	0.891	0.990
Saturated model	1.000		1.000		1.000
Independence model	0.000	0.000	0.000	0.000	0.000

Parsimony-adjusted measures			
Model	PRATIO	PNFI	PCFI
Default model	0.095	0.094	0.094
Saturated model	0.000	0.000	0.000
Independence model	1.000	0.000	0.000

NCP			
Model	NCP	LO 90	HI 90
Default model	33.006	17.396	56.043
Saturated model	0.000	0.000	0.000
Independence model	3166.100	2984.268	3355.226

© The Editor(s) (if applicable) and The Author(s) 2020
B. Kodden, *The Art of Sustainable Performance*, SpringerBriefs in Business,
https://doi.org/10.1007/978-3-030-46463-9

FMIN

Model	FMIN	FO	LO 90	HI 90
Default model	0.031	0.029	0.016	0.050
Saturated model	0.000	0.000	0.000	0.000
Independence model	2.843	2.824	2.662	2.993

RMSEA

Model	PRATIO	PNFI	PCFI	
Default model	0.121	0.088	0.158	0.000
Independence model	0.367	0.356	0.378	0.000

Tools

In this chapter, you will find the different tools that you can use (for yourself and your organization) to achieve sustainable performance.

The first is a Checklist Recruitment and Selection that is based on the performance indicators that this study found to be the most important. There are also several questionnaires regarding the most important performance criteria and personality traits. By filling these out for yourself, you can determine your level of self-efficacy, work engagement, and adaptability. You can also use them to evaluate others.

The Tools chapter ends with examples of the STAR methods and its successors, STARR (Knegtman 2016) and STARRA.

Reference

Knegtmans R (2016) Agile Talent. Negen cruciale stappen bij de selectie van het toptalent van morgen. Business Contact, Amsterdam

Checklist Recruitment and Selection

In this checklist, you can use your own preferred scoring system. For example, 1 = very low, 5 = very high, or, 1 = very bad, 10 = excellent. Keep in mind that not every position in every organization at any moment should attach the same value to a certain personality trait. That is why you can enter your own value in column A: Value. If you do not want to assign an exceptional value to any one of the criteria, you can enter a 1 for all of them in column A. This way, you will give all nine performance criteria from this study the same weight. If, however, you want to emphasize specific performance criteria for a particular vacancy, then you can increase the value in column A.

By multiplying the scores from column A (Value) with the scores in B (Evaluation), you end up with a rating (column C). Using the results, you can determine for yourself whether or not a candidate meets your requirements.

	Selection criterion	Value (A)	Evaluation (B)	Rating $A \times B$ (C)
1	Self-efficacy			
2	Adaptability			
3	Fit with mental job requirements			
4	Intrinsic motivation			
5	Intelligence			
6	Vigor			
7	Dedication			
8	Fit with supervisor			
9	Talent			
10	Total			

Questionnaire Self-efficacy (Bandura 1977)

Please indicate to what extent the following statements apply to you (between 1 and 4):

No.	Statement	Completely incorrect	Barely correct	Somewhat correct	Completely correct
		Score			
1	I always manage to solve difficult problems when I make enough of an effort	1	2	3	4
2	Even when people are working against me, I always manage to find ways to get what I want	1	2	3	4
3	I find it easy to stick to my plans and achieve my goal	1	2	3	4

(continued)

(continued)

No.	Statement	Completely incorrect	Barely correct	Somewhat correct	Completely correct
		Score			
4	I am confident that I can effectively handle unexpected events	1	2	3	4
5	Thanks to my resourcefulness, I know how to act in unexpected situations	1	2	3	4
6	I can solve most problems when I make enough of an effort	1	2	3	4
7	I stay calm when I am confronted with a difficult situation because I am confident about my problem-solving skills	1	2	3	4
8	When I am confronted with a problem, I usually know multiple solutions for it	1	2	3	4
9	I usually know what to do when I am in a difficult situation	1	2	3	4
10	Whatever happens, I will deal with it	1	2	3	4

Norm score (Own interpretation)

Self-efficacy
Totals statements $1 - 10 = \ldots$ divided by $10 = \ldots$

Reference

Bandura A (1977 Self-efficacy: toward a unifying theory of behavioral change. Psychol Rev 84(2):191–215

Questionnaire Adaptability (Cozijnsen and Vrakking 2013)

Please indicate to what extent the following statements apply to you (between 1 and 4, beware: reversed rating):

		Fully agree	Partially agree	Partially disagree	Fully disagree
No.	Statement	Score			
1	I get frustrated by change	1	2	3	4
2	I look forward to changes at work	1	2	3	4
3	I am usually resistant to change	1	2	3	4
4	The management of the organization profits most from changes, unlike the employees	1	2	3	4
5	I am always inclined to try new ideas	1	2	3	4
6	I am usually supportive of new ideas	1	2	3	4
7	I find most changes to be pleasant	1	2	3	4
8	Change usually helps improve unsatisfactory situations at work	1	2	3	4
9	I am usually hesitant to try out new ideas	1	2	3	4

Norm score (own interpretation)

Adaptability
Totals statements 1 through 9 = … divided by 9 = …

Reference

Cozijnsen AJ, Vrakking WJ (2013) Basisboek veranderkunde. Kluwer, Deventer

Questionnaire Work Engagement (Bakker et al. 2009)

Please indicate to what extent the following statements apply to you (between 0 and 6):

No.	Statement	Never Score	Rarely	Sometimes	Usually	Often	Very often	Always
1	I feel full of energy at work	0	1	2	3	4	5	6
2	I think the work I do is useful and meaningful	0	1	2	3	4	5	6
3	Time flies when I am at work	0	1	2	3	4	5	6
4	I feel fit and strong when I work	0	1	2	3	4	5	6
5	I am enthusiastic about my job	0	1	2	3	4	5	6
6	When I am working, I forget everything around me	0	1	2	3	4	5	6
7	My work inspires me	0	1	2	3	4	5	6

(continued)

(continued)

No.	Statement	Score	Never	Rarely	Sometimes	Usually	Often	Very often	Always
8	I am looking forward to going to work when I wake up		0	1	2	3	4	5	6
9	I feel happy when I am working very hard		0	1	2	3	4	5	6
10	I am proud of my job		0	1	2	3	4	5	6
11	My work absorbs me completely		0	1	2	3	4	5	6
12	When I am working, I can go on for a very long time		0	1	2	3	4	5	6
13	My work is a challenge to me		0	1	2	3	4	5	6
14	My work moves me		0	1	2	3	4	5	6
15	I have strong mental resilience at my work		0	1	2	3	4	5	6

Norm scores

Vigor
Totals statements $1 + 4 + 8 + 12 + 15 = \ldots$ divided by 5 = ...

Dedication
Totals statements $2 + 5 + 7 + 10 + 13 = \ldots$ divided by 5 = ...

Absorption
Totals statements $3 + 6 + 9 + 11 + 14 = \ldots$ divided by 5 = ...

Work Engagement
Totals statements 1 through $15 = \ldots$ divided by 15 = ...

Reference

Bakker A, Schaufeli W, Van Rhenen W (2009) How changes in job demands and resources predict burnout, work engagement, and sickness absenteeism. J Organ Behav

The STAR and STARR(A) Methods

Entrepreneurs, supervisors, and HR officers can use these questionnaires as an inspiration for asking specific questions during the structured interview, for instance, by using the STAR method. The STAR method is a commonly used and proven interview technique to evaluate the qualities of an applicant. STAR stands for Situation, Task, Action, Result.

For instance, if you wanted to evaluate the level of self-efficacy of an applicant, you could use the following method:

Question 1 (also see statement 1 of the Self-Efficacy Questionnaire)
(To be asked by the interviewer and answered by applicant)

- *Situation*: Think of a situation during your career so far when you encountered significant work-related problems but were able to solve these because you made enough of an effort. Try to present the best possible example of yourself when answering this question.
- *Task*: Give a brief description of the situation, preferably including the main problem. Explain your task or role in the situation as clearly as possible.
- *Action*: Name the things that you actually did in order to solve the problem, meaning your own, concrete actions.
- *Result*: Name the final results and your role in them!

Question 2 (also see statement 2 of the Self-Efficacy Questionnaire)
(To be asked by the interviewer and answered by applicant)

- *Situation*: Think of a situation during your career when someone was actively working against you, but you still managed to find a way to get what you wanted. Try to present the best possible example of yourself when answering this question.
- *Task*: Give a brief description of the situation, preferably including the main problem. Explain your task or role in the situation as clearly as possible.
- *Action*: Name the things that you actually did in order to solve the problem, meaning your own, concrete actions.
- *Result*: Name the final results and your role in them!

Rating
Rate all the answers. For instance, using:

- 5 full self-efficacy;
- 4 good self-efficacy;
- 3 sufficient self-efficacy;

- 2 some self-efficacy;
- 1 very little self-efficacy.

This will provide a complete picture of the candidate's self-efficacy. By using this approach for the other performance criteria and personality traits, you will end up with a structured overview of the overall quality of the applicant.

The STARR and STARRA Methods
You can add an extra step to the STAR method for selecting the right employee. You can do this by adding an extra element to STAR, the "R" for Reflection (Knegtmans 2016).

- *Reflection*: What did you learn from the situation? Knowing what you know now, what would you have done differently? What did it teach you about yourself? What would you change in the future?

In his book, *Agile Talent* (2016), Knegtmans adds yet another step. He expands the STARR method with a sixth element; the "A" for "Adapt" (the STARRA method)

- *Adapt*: What did you subsequently do with the reflection? How did you implement what you learned? How did your analysis lead to concrete and measurable new behavior or approaches?

Reference

Knegtmans R (2016) Agile talent. Negen cruciale stappen bij de selectie van het toptalent van morgen. Business Contact, Amsterdam

Sources of Inspiration

Ankersen R (2012) The gold mine effect. Crack the secrets of high performance. Icon Books, London

Bakker A, Schaufeli WB, Leiter MP, Taris TW (2008) Work engagement: an emerging concept in occupational health psychology. Work Stress 22(3)

Bakker A, Schaufeli W, Van Rhenen W (2009) How changes in job demands and resources predict burnout, work engagement, and sickness absenteeism. J Organ Behav

Bandura A (1977) Self-efficacy: toward a unifying theory of behavioral change. Psychol Rev 84(2):191–215

Baumeister RF, Tierney J (2012) Willpower. Why self-control is the secret to success

Beer M, Nohria N (2000). Cracking the code of change. Harvard Business Review, 78(2):133–141

Blomme R, Kodden B (2014) Engagement: a new concept in the hospitality industry? The role of management in increasing engagement amongst hospitality workers. The Routledge Handbook of Hospitality Management 85–93

Boswell J (1791) The life of Samuel Johnson. The librarian of Alexandria. Penguin Classics, London/New York

Braun D, Kramer J (2016) The corporate t: organizational lessons froms anthropology. Routledge

Bregman R (2016) Weg met controle. Leve de intrinsiek gemotiveerde mens. De Correspondent, 18 October 2016. Consulted at www.decorrespondent.nl

Buckingham M, Clifton DO (2006) Ontdek je sterke punten. Utrecht: Het Spectrum

Burnes B (2004) Managing Change (4th edn). Financial Times/Prentice Hall, Harlow

Cameron KS, Quinn RE (1988) Paradox and transformation: toward a theory of change in organization and management. Ballinger, Cambrdige, MA

CBS (2015) Eén op de zeven werknemers heeft burn-outklachten. https://www.cbs.nl/nl-nl/nieuws/2015/47/cbs-en-tno-een-op-de-zeven-werknemers-heeft-burn-outklachten

Childress JR, Senn LE (1995) In the eye of the storm. Leadership Press, Los Angeles, CA

Cohen PR, Feigenbaum EA (2014) The handbook of artificial intelligence. HeurisTech Press, Stanford, CA;William Kaufmann, Inc., Stanford, CA

Collins J (2001) Good to great. Why some companies make the leap … and others don't. Harper Collins Publishers, New York, NY

Collins J (2009) Waarom sommige bedrijven een sprong vooruit maken … en an- dere niet. Business Contact, Amsterdam

Colvin G (2010) Talent is overrated. Penguin Group, New York, NY

Cozijnsen AJ, Vrakking WJ (2013) Basisboek Veranderkunde, Kluwer, Deventer

Crwys-Williams J (2011) Nelson Mandela—citaten. Het Spectrum, Houten

Csikszentmihalyi M (1975) Beyond boredom and anxiety. Jossey-Bass Publishers, San Francisco, CA

Csikszentmihalyi M (2007) Flow. Psychologie van de optimale ervaring. Boom, Amsterdam

Csikszentmihalyi M, LeFevre J (1989) Optimal experience in work and leisure. J Personal Soc Psychol 56(5):815–822

Deci EL, Ryan RM (1985) Intrinsic motivation and self-determination in hu- man behavior. Plenum, New York, NY

Deci EL, Ryan RM (2000) The 'what' and 'why' of goal pursuits: human needs and the self-determination of behavior. Psychol Inq 11(4):227–268

DeVoe S, Pfeffer J (2011) Time is tight: how higher economic value of time increases feelings of time pressure. J Appl Psychol 96(4):665–676. Doi 10.1037/a0022148

Diehl PJ, Stoffelsen JM (2007) Vitaliteit en arbeid in 100 vragen. Kluwer, Alphen aan den Rijn

Pink D (2009) The suprising truth about what motivates us. Riverhead Books

Ehrhart KH, Ziegert JC (2005) Why are individuals attracted to organizations? J Manag 31(6):901–919

Ericsson KA (ed) (2014) The road to excellence: the acquisition of expert performance in the arts and sciences, sports, and games. Psychology Press, New York, NY

Ericsson KA (2016) Peak: secrets from the new science of expertise. Houghton Mifflin Harcourt, Boston, MA

Ernst & Young (2017) A global study on work-life challenges across generations. https://www.ey.com/Publication/vwLUAssets/Global_generations_study/%24FILE/EY-global-generations-a-global-study-on-work-life-challenges-across-generations.pdf

Evans D (2012) Risk Intelligence. How to live with uncertainty. Free Press, Florence, MA

Feser C (2011) Serial innovators. Firms that change the world. Wiley, Hoboken, NJ

Frankl V (1946) Man's search for meaning. The classic tribute to hope from the Holocaust

Friedman WJ (2011) The Zeigarnik effect and completing everything. http://www.willjoelfriedman.com/listArticles.html

Gagné M, Deci EL (2005) Self-determination theory and work motivation. J Organ Behav 26(4):331–362

Gagné M, Forest J, Vansteenkiste M, Crevier-Braud L, Van den Broeck A, Aspeli AK et al (2010) Validation evidence in ten languages for the revised motivation at work scale. Concordia University, Montreal

Gallup (2013) Worldwide, 13% of Employees Are Engaged at Work. http://www.gallup.com/poll/165269/worldwide-employees-engaged-work.aspx

Galton F (2018) Hereditary character and t. Suzeteo Publishers

Gladwell M (2005) Blink: the power of thinking without thinking. Little, Brown and Company, New York, NY

Gladwell M (2009) Outliers: the story of success. Little, Brown and Company, New York, NY

Grant A (2013) Give and take: why helping others drives our success. Penguin Books, New York, NY

Grant A (2016) Originals: how non-conformists move the world. Viking, New York, NY

Grimberg M (2012) Van talent naar high performer. Consulted at http://vds.nl/blog/van-talent-naar-high-performer/

Groot de A (1946) Het denken van den schaker: argumenten voor een nieuwe traditie. Noord-Hollandse Uitgevers mij

Groot de A, Gobel F (1996) Perception and memory in chess: Heuristics of the professional eye. Van Gorcum Assen

Hammer M (1996) Beyond reengineering: how the proces-centered organization is changing our lives. Harper Business, New York, NY

Howe MJA, Davidson JW, Sloboda JA (1998) Innate talents: teality or myth? Behav Brain Sci 21(3)

Huang T, Larsen KT, Möller NC, Andersen LB (2013) The effects of physical activity and exercise on brain-derived neurotrophic factor in healthy humans: a review

Kerr J (2013) Legacy. What the all blacks can teach us about the business of life. Constable & Robinson Ltd., London

Knegtmans R (2016). Agile talent. Negen cruciale stappen bij de selectie van het toptalent van morgen. Business Contact, Amsterdam

Kodden SFGP (2011) Dedication. Nyenrode Business Universiteit

Kodden S (2014) Be a HERO. How to bring out leadership in everyone. Bernard Daniel Press

Kodden B, Groenweg B (2019) The mediating effect of work engagement on the relationship between person-organization fit and knowledge sharing. J Appl Bus Econ 21(8)

Kodden B, Hupkes L (2019) Organizational environment, personal resources and work engagement as predictors of coaching performance. J Manag Policy Pract 20(3). https://doi.org/10.33423/jmpp.v20i3.2230

Kodden B, Roelofs J (2019). Psychological contract as a mediator of the leadership-turn over intentions relationship. J Organ Psychol 19(2). https://doi.org/10.33423/jop.v19i2.2046

Kodden B, Ingen van R (2019) Knowledge productivity in the 2020s: time for a new ERA. J Appl Bus Econ 21(4). https://doi.org/10.33423/jabe.v21i4.2132

Kotter JP (1995). Leading change: why transformation efforts fail. Harvard Bus Rev 73(2):59-67

Kristof AL (1996) Person-organization fit: an integrative review of its conceptualizations, measurement and implications. Person Psychol 49(1), March, 1–49

Kristof-Brown AL, Jansen KJ, Colbert AE (2002) A policy-capturing study of the simultaneous effects of fit with jobs, groups and organizations. J Appl Psychol 87(5):985–993

Lewin K (1951) Field theory in social science; selected theoretical papers (ed. D. Cartwright). Harper & Row, New York, NY

Lewis M (2003) Moneyball. The art of winning an unfair game. Writers House, New York, NY

Loflin J (2014) Improving your productivity: the zeigarnik effect. Consulted at http://www.jonesloflin.com/jonesloflinblog/improving-your-productivity-the-Zeigarnik-effect/9222014

Mackenbach J (2010) Ziekte in Nederland. Gezondheid tussen politiek en biologie. Elsevier Gezondheidszorg, Amsterdam

Macnamara B, Moreau D, Hambrick DZ (2016) The relationship between de liberate practice and performance in sports. A meta-analysis. Persp Psychol Sci 11(3):333–350

Martin J, Schmidt C (2010) How to keep your top talent. Harvard Business Review, May, Number 5

Masicampo EJ, Baumeister RF (2011) Consider it done! Plan making can eli minate the cognitive effects of unfulfilled goals. J Person Social Psychol 101(4):October, 667–683. Advance online publication. Doi 10.1037/a0024192

Maslow AH (1943) A theory of human motivation. Psychol Rev 50(4):370–396. Consulted at psychclassics.yorku.ca

McGraw KO, Fiala J (1982) Undermining the zeigarnik effect. J Person 50(1):58–65

Meijers J (2016) Talent? Vooral hard blijven doorwerken. Consulted at https://d.nl/morgen/1153168/talent-vooral-hard-blijven-doorwerken

Peters T (2005) Leadership. DK Publishers

Peters T (1982) In search of excellence: lessons from America's best-run companies. Harper Collins, New York, NY

Pink D (2011) Drive. The surprising truth about what motivates us. Riverhead Books

Ployhart RE, Bliese PD (2006) Individual adaptability (I-ADAPT) theory: conceptualizing the antecedents, consequences, and measurement of individual differences in adaptability. In: Burke CS, Pierce LG, Salas E (eds) Understanding adaptability: a prerequisite for effective performance within complex environments, vol 6, St. Louis, MO, Elsevier Science, pp 3–39

Rachman S (1989) Fear and courage. W.H. Freeman, New York, NY

Rammeloo E (2016) Chinezen azen op plekje aan Amerikaanse universiteit. De Tijd, 9 June. Consulted at www.detijd.be

Rek de W (2012) Train uw wilskracht. de Volkskrant, 12 May. Consulted at http://www.volkskrant.nl/archief/-train-uw-wilskracht~a3254500/

Rhenen van W (2008) From stress to engagement (thesis University of Amsterdam). Consulted at http://dare.uva.nl/document/107037

Ryan RM, Deci EL (2000) Self-determination theory and the facilitation of intrinsic motivation, social development, and well-being. American Psychologist 55(1):68–78

Ryan RM, Deci EL (2000) Intrinsic and extrinsic motivations: classic definitions and new directions. Contemp Educ Psychol 25:54–67. Doi 10.1006/ceps.1999.1020

Ryan RM, Frederick C (1997) On energy, personality, and health: subjective vitality as a dynamic reflection of well-being. J Person 65(3):529–565

Schaufeli WB, Taris TW (2005) The conceptualization and measurement of burnout: common ground and worlds apart. Work Stress 19(3):256–262

Schaufeli BW, Bakker BA (2003) Occupational health psychology. Unit. Utrecht University

Schaufeli WB, Bakker AB (2007) Burnout en bevlogenheid. In: WB Schaufeli, Bakker AB (eds) De psychologie van arbeid en gezondheid, Bohn Stafleu van Loghum, Houten, pp 341–358

Schmidt F, Hunter J (1998) The validity and utility of selection methods in per- sonnel psychology: practical and theoretical implications of 85 years of re- search findings. Psychol Bull 124(2):262–274

Schwarz T (2012) The magic of doing one thing at a time. Consulted at http://blogs.hbr.org/2012/03/the-magic-of-doing-one-thing-a/

Schwarz B (2016) Waarom we werken. Amsterdam University Press, Amsterdam

Schwarzer R, Schmitz GS, Daytner GT (1999) The teacher self-efficacy scale [online publication]. Retrieved from http://userpage.fu-berlin.de/~health/teacher_se.htm

Seidell J (2012) Sporten maakt je slim? In broadcast: https://www.bnr.nl/ra-dio/10178252/sporten-maakt-je-slim?disableUserNav=true

Sengupta K, Abdel-Hamid TK, Van Wassenhove LN (2008) The Experience Trap. Harvard Bus Rev 86(2), February, 94–101

Sinek S (2009) Start with why. Penguin Books Ltd., New York

Sluis van der LEC (2008) Talent management in strategisch perspectief. Nyenrode Business University, Breukelen

Sluis van der LEC, Berkhout B (2009) Nederland Talentenland. Themanummer Develop 1:1–7

Stajkovic AD, Bandura A, Locke EA, Lee D, Sergent K (2018) Test of three conceptual models of influence of the big five personality traits and self-efficacy on academic performance: a meta-analytic path-analysis. Personal Indiv Diff 120:238–245

Storm K, Rothmann S (2003) A psychometric analysis of the utrecht work engagement scale in the South African police service. SA J Industr Psychol 29(4):62–70

Strauss K, Griffin MA, Parker SK (2015). Building and sustaining proactive behaviors: the role of adaptivity and job satisfaction. J Bus Psychol 30(1), March, 63–72

Strijk JE, Proper KI, Beek AJ van der, Mechelen W van (2009) The Vital@ Work Study. The systematic development of a lifestyle intervention to improve older workers' vitality and the design of a randomised controlled trial evalua- ting this intervention. BMC Public Health, 9(1), 408

Syed M (2011 Bounce: the myth of talent and the power of practice. Estate, London

Taris R (2003) Person-environment fit. A longitudinal study of the interaction between employee characteristics and work environmental characteristics. Ridderprint Offsetdrukkerij, Ridderkerk

UvA (2008) Personeelsselectie in tijden van krapte. Onderzoek door UvA en Randstad). Diemen

Vergouw G (2014) Bondscoach! Coaching handboek voor 16 miljoen Nederlanders

Vuuren T van (2011) Je hoeft niet ziek te zijn om beter te worden (oration). Open University Heerlen, Heerlen

Walsh B (2010) The score takes care of itself: my philosophy on leadership. Portfolio, New York

Wiese L, Rothmann S, Storm K (2003) Coping, stress and burnout in the South African police service in Kwazulu-natal. SA J Indust Psychol

Wilkins KG, Santilli S, Ferrari L, Nota L, Tracey TJG, Soresi S (2014) The relationship among positive emotional dispositions, career adaptability, and satisfaction in Italian high school students. J. Vocat. Behav. 85, 329–338. 10.1016/j.jvb.2014.08.004

Wolf, L. de (2012). Help! Mijn batterijen lopen leeg - Een burn-out krijg je niet alleen, kies voor je talent. Lannoo Campus, Tielt (B)

World Economic Forum (2016) The future of jobs. Consulted at https://www.weforum.org/reports/the-future-of-jobs

Woods E (1997) Training a tiger. Harper Collins

Xanthopoulou D, Bakker AB, Heuven E, Demerouti E, Schaufeli WB (2008a) Working in the sky: a diary study among flight attendants. J Occup Health Psychol 13(4):345–356.

Xanthopoulou D, Bakker AB, Demerouti E, Schaufeli WB (2008b). How job and personal resources influence work engagement and financial returns: a diary study in a Greek fast-food company. J Occup Organ Psychol 82(1):183–200

Zeigarnik B (1927) Das Behalten erledigter und unerledigter Handlungen. Psychologische Forschung, 9:1–85

Zhou M, Lin W (2016). Adaptability and life satisfaction: the moderating role of social support. Frontiers in Psychology

Zigarelli MA (2011) The Messiah-method: the seven disciplines of the winningest college program in America

Glossary

Adaptability The willingness to change and ability adapt to a changing environment, work methods, work hours, tasks, responsibilities, and the behavior of others.

Absorption Being completely engrossed in one's work in a pleasant way, becoming so absorbed by it that one forgets the time and finds it difficult to detach.

Dedication A strong involvement with one's work; it is seen as both useful and meaningful, inspiring, and challenging, and it generates feelings of pride and enthusiasm.

Extrinsic motivation Motivation to work that comes from external sources like the prospect of a reward or a penalty for a certain action because it offers a certain standard of living. Doing a job because the salary is good.

Intelligence Mental capacity, the ability to apply knowledge and experience to solve problems.

Intrinsic motivation Motivation to work that comes from within because someone really enjoys his or her job, has fun doing it and finds pleasurable moments in one's work.

Mental job requirements The aspects of the job that require regular psychological (cognitive and emotional) effort, and therefore have certain physical and/or psychological costs.

Optimism Having a positive attitude to life and believing that everything will turn out fine.

Organizational culture The collection of norms, values, and behaviors that are shared by an organization's members and that connect them to each other and the organization.

Physical job requirements The aspects of the job that require regular physical effort, and therefore have certain physical and/or psychological costs.

Self-esteem The image a person has of him or herself, regardless of reason or logic.

Self-control The ability to control one's impulses and whims. Not doing something now because it conflicts with what you want to achieve in the long term.

Self-efficacy Thinking one has the skills to perform a certain task and the confidence in one's ability to successfully complete it. Different from self-confidence in that

© The Editor(s) (if applicable) and The Author(s) 2020
B. Kodden, *The Art of Sustainable Performance*, SpringerBriefs in Business,
https://doi.org/10.1007/978-3-030-46463-9

the latter refers to confidence in oneself, whereas self-efficacy is about believing that one has the necessary skills to perform a certain task.

Self-confidence The belief that one can successfully influence and control one's surroundings.

Stress resistance Being able to continue to perform effectively under a deadline, despite setbacks or disappointments.

Sustainable performance Being able to continually achieve personal and team objectives.

Talent The natural ability and innate aptitude to excel in one's job.

Vigor Having a lot of energy, feeling fit and strong, being able to work long hours without getting tired, and having strong mental resilience and perseverance.

Work engagement A positive, affective-cognitive state of supreme satisfaction, characterized by vigor, dedication, and absorption.

Willingness to change A positive behavioral intention of an employee regarding the introduction of changes in the structure, culture, or work methods of an organization or department, resulting in an effort by the employee to speed up and/or support the chance process.

Willpower The will to persevere and the capacity to control oneself.